THE NOT SO BIG HOUSE

THE NOT SO

Sarah Susanka with Kira Obolensky

BIG HOUSE

A Blueprint for the Way We Really Live

The Taunton Press

Cover photo: George Heinrich
(Architects: Michaela Mahady and Wayne Branum)

The Taunton Press
Inspiration for hands-on living®

Text © 2001 by Sarah Susanka
Photos © 2001 by The Taunton Press, Inc., where noted
Printed in the United States of America
10 9

The Taunton Press, Inc., 63 South Main Street, PO Box 5506, Newtown, CT 06470-5506
e-mail: tp@taunton.com

The Not So Big House was originally published in hardcover in 1998 by The Taunton Press, Inc.

Library of Congress Cataloging-in Publication Data

Susanka, Sarah.
    The not so big house : a blueprint for the way we really live /
Sarah Susanka with Kira Obolensky.
        p. cm.
    Includes bibliographical references and index.
    ISBN 1-56158-130-5 (hardcover)
    ISBN 1-56158-376-6 (softcover)
    1. Architecture, Domestic—Psychological aspects.   2. Space
(Architecture).   3. Interior architecture—Psychological aspects.
I. Obolensky, Kira.   II. Title.
NA7125.S87   1998
728'.37—dc21   98-23080

For our grandchildren

A c k n o w l e d g

University of California, Berkeley. Their remarkable book, *A Pattern Language*, published in 1977, struck me early in my education as the most appropriate way to think about architectural design, buildings, and the people who inhabit them. It is largely as a result of their work, which has provided inspiration for a generation of architects, that I came to write my own book.

Next, I want to thank all my partners and colleagues at Mulfinger, Susanka, Mahady & Partners. There's a firmly held myth in the architecture profession that you can't make a living designing homes. The success of our firm is living proof that you can. Most of the images in the book come from the work of my colleagues. The individuals responsible for each project illustrated, together with the names of the photographers, are listed in the credits at the back of the book. Without their creativity and dedication to good design, this book would have been greatly diminished.

I also want to thank architect Robert Gerloff, once an associate with our firm and now in practice for himself. Robert wrote a pivotal article in the 1980s for our local AIA Chapter magazine, *Archi-*

W henever I pick up a book for the first time, I turn straight to the acknowledgments. I'm always impressed by all the people who have provided inspiration and helped the author assemble the tome in hand. Now, as I near the end of this book's production, I too am in a position to extend thanks to all those who have made this book possible.

First, I wish to acknowledge the debt I owe to Christopher Alexander and his colleagues at the

ments

tecture Minnesota. In the article, entitled "Bigger Isn't (necessarily) Better," he identified a theme that has become a guiding light for our firm. Although we take on projects of all shapes and sizes, it was Robert's insightful article that made us realize we could interest our clients in houses with less square footage built with more care and detail.

A very special thank you to Balthazar and Monica Korab, who very kindly supplied images of some of the landmark homes presented here of Frank Lloyd Wright, Greene and Greene, and Le Corbusier. Balthazar Korab is one of the premier architectural photographers of his generation, as well as the father of Christian Korab, whose photographs also appear throughout the book.

My admiration for the spatial qualities of Prairie School architecture led me to the work of E. Fay Jones, whose houses and chapels sing with a beauty that radiates from within. He inspired me to follow my heart and design homes that put their emphasis on beauty and habitability, rather than on uniqueness. He taught me that it is only through standing on the shoulders of those masters who have gone before that we can really learn our craft. His humility and gentle encouragement of young architects around the country have been of enormous value.

In the actual making of the book, I want to thank all the people at The Taunton Press who helped me through the process. Together with friend, playwright, and freelance writer Kira Obolensky, we all worked long and hard to make this not only a beautiful book but also one filled with ideas to help change the way we design and build houses today. Kira helped craft my original manuscript into a far more accessible and readable volume; a better writing partner would have been hard to find.

And finally, I must thank all the clients and friends who graciously allowed us to use images of their homes to illustrate the ideas in this book, as well as all the builders and craftspeople whose work made each house sing. Every concept described in this book evolved out of a need to find a solution to a problem presented by a client or clients over the past 15 years. Through their generosity, others are being given the opportunity to learn from their experiences. Thank you all, and may your homes live up to your dreams and continue to nurture the lives of your families for many decades to come. ■

Contents

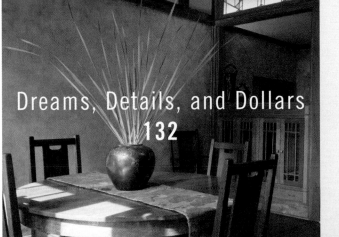

Introduction

The idea of a Not So Big House, a house that favors the quality of its space over the quantity, has evolved during the 15 years I've practiced architecture in the Twin Cities. Maybe it was the 1980s that created what I call the "starter castle" complex—the notion that houses should be designed to impress rather than nurture. More rooms, bigger spaces, and vaulted ceilings do not necessarily give us what we need in a home. And when the impulse for big spaces is combined with outdated patterns of home design and building, the result is more often than not a house that doesn't work.

When my husband and I, both of us architects, were planning our new house, we knew that we wanted a home that would inspire us and make the best use of the money we had to spend. Whatever we ended up with, we wanted our house to express the way we actually live. We started the planning process by considering an addition to our two-story 1904 four-square. We're not formal people, and the separation between kitchen and living space meant that we spent all our time in the kitchen—the tiniest room in the house. To change that, however, we would have had to add more space, which would have made our house bigger while leaving half of it still unused. That option didn't seem sensible. In fact, it seemed downright wasteful.

I quickly realized that our old house was designed for a pattern of life that was fundamentally different from the way we live today. So we decided to design our own house—which would be Not So Big—with each space in use every day. And it would be beautiful. I've designed big houses that are beautiful and small houses that had tight budgets; I wanted our house to combine the beauty of the big house with the efficiency of the small one. Rather than spend our budget on square footage we wouldn't use, we decided to put the money toward making the house an expression of our personalities.

We knew that by building such a house we would be going out on a limb, because the institutions that dictate the value and resale of houses demand all

the extra spaces that we knew we would never use. When we met with the banker and explained that our new house would have no formal dining room, he was dubious. But as I described to him my frustration with designing large houses with rarely used formal spaces, and my vision to put forward a different home model into the marketplace, his demeanor completely changed. Suddenly, he was telling us

about his own house, a suburban Colonial, and admitting that in 25 years his family had never sat in the living room. They lived in their family room. The banker, who at first appeared to be our biggest obstacle, became our strongest advocate.

So we built our house, and along the way many of the ideas that had been percolating in my subconscious came into being. I began to speak locally and nationally about the concept of the Not So Big House and found an extraordinary amount of confirmation from audiences. Even realtors, who perpetuate the conventional wisdom of resale requirements, were excited by the concept of building Not So Big. In fact, two realtors—a husband and wife team—approached me after one lecture and asked that I design a Not So Big House for them.

This book contains the work of more than 35 architects and related professionals who I have had the privilege of working with in our architectural firm in Minnesota. These colleagues have worked with more than 3,000 residential clients over the past 15 years. As a result of all this work, we get to see the aspirations, the struggles, the needs, and the realities of people who want new or remodeled homes. Architects build dreams, but we also have to help clients reconcile those dreams with real budgets. A house that favors quality of design over

quantity of space satisfies people with big dreams and not so big budgets far more so than a house with those characteristics in reverse.

It's time for a different kind of house. A house that is more than square footage; a house that is Not So Big, where each room is used every day. A house with a floorplan inspired by our informal lifestyle instead of the way our grandparents lived. A house for the future that embraces a few well-worn concepts from the past. A house that expresses our values and our personalities. It's time for the Not So Big House.

The Not So Big House isn't just a small house. Rather, it's a smaller house, filled with special details and designed to accommodate the lifestyles of its occupants. I've discovered living in my own Not So Big House that the quality of my life has improved. I'm surrounded in my home by beautiful forms, lots of daylight, natural materials, and the things that I love. Our house fits us perfectly and is unabashedly comfortable. My house feeds my spirit, and it is with this insight that I share with you how to make your house do the same. ■

For our grandchildren

A c k n o w l e d g

University of California, Berkeley. Their remarkable book, *A Pattern Language*, published in 1977, struck me early in my education as the most appropriate way to think about architectural design, buildings, and the people who inhabit them. It is largely as a result of their work, which has provided inspiration for a generation of architects, that I came to write my own book.

Next, I want to thank all my partners and colleagues at Mulfinger, Susanka, Mahady & Partners. There's a firmly held myth in the architecture profession that you can't make a living designing homes. The success of our firm is living proof that you can. Most of the images in the book come from the work of my colleagues. The individuals responsible for each project illustrated, together with the names of the photographers, are listed in the credits at the back of the book. Without their creativity and dedication to good design, this book would have been greatly diminished.

I also want to thank architect Robert Gerloff, once an associate with our firm and now in practice for himself. Robert wrote a pivotal article in the 1980s for our local AIA Chapter magazine, *Archi-*

Whenever I pick up a book for the first time, I turn straight to the acknowledgments. I'm always impressed by all the people who have provided inspiration and helped the author assemble the tome in hand. Now, as I near the end of this book's production, I too am in a position to extend thanks to all those who have made this book possible.

First, I wish to acknowledge the debt I owe to Christopher Alexander and his colleagues at the

"Not everything that can be counted counts, and not everything that counts can be counted."—Albert Einstein

So many houses, so big with so little soul. Our suburbs are filled with houses that are bigger than ever. But are bigger houses really better? Are the dreams that build them bigger, or is it simply that there seems to be no alternative? Americans are searching for home in unprecedented numbers. Yet when we look, the only tools we seem to have are those we find in the real estate listings. But a house is more than square footage and the number of beds and baths. In one of the wealthiest societies ever, many people are deeply dissatisfied with their most expensive purchase. Which is where Paul and Laura come in.

I had just completed a lecture at our local Home and Garden Show. As I stepped from the podium, I was greeted by several members of the audience who wanted to thank me for saying something they hadn't heard before—that we need to value quality over quantity in house design. There was a couple in the crowd with a story about their own experience, a story that gave me the impetus

A Not So Big House exchanges space for soul, so that the quality of the space is more important than the sheer square footage.

Rather than spend their budget on spaces they never use, people who build Not So Big tailor their houses to fit their lives.

to write this book. As they approached me, I saw tears in the woman's eyes.

"We want you to come to our new house and tell us what you think," she said. "We just built it. We spent over $500,000 on it and we hate it. It's just not us at all. After listening to you, we think…" She paused and looked at her husband, who nodded. "We *know* that we have to start over. All we've got is square footage with no soul. We want the type of house that you describe. Can you help us?"

The next week, I drove out to the suburbs to see the house, past row after row of enormous structures covering the newly developed hillsides. These houses loomed in their treeless sites, staring blankly out toward vistas of more of the same. I felt as though I was driving through a collection of massive storage containers for people.

Paul and Laura's house was fairly typical of new, large subdivision homes. It had the required arched window topping off a soaring front entrance scaled more for an office building than a home. Inside the house, I was greeted by an enormous space, all white, with a cold marble floor. There was no separation between this vaulting foyer and the next room, which I assumed must be the family room, although there was no furniture in it (see the photo on p. 10). Laura ushered me into the kitchen, which was also oversized and made up of all hard surfaces that gave it the acoustics of a parking garage.

She and Paul explained to me that until a year before, they had lived in the city, in a small, older home. Although they liked the house, their three boys were growing up quickly, and they were starting to feel cramped for space. The house had no family room, so the kids didn't have a place to be rambunctious. The couple found a piece of property they loved. The lot was owned by a builder, who made it clear as part of the terms of sale that he would be the one to build the home. They thought this would be fine—they didn't know any other builders and this one had a good reputation.

American suburbs are filled with big, expensive houses, but a bigger house isn't necessarily a better home.

The builder showed them his portfolio of plans and explained that they could choose any one of them. Although they weren't particularly enamored with any of the plans, they picked the one that seemed to have the rooms they needed in the right relationships to one another: kitchen opening into family room, formal living room separated from family room to allow kids some space to play away from mom and dad.

It wasn't until the house was actually under construction that the feeling of uneasiness began to set in. As the framing proceeded, the heights of the spaces became clear, as did the proportions of each room. "All the rooms just seemed huge," said Laura. They asked to make some changes, such as lowering some ceiling heights and dividing a room in two to make each a more manageable scale. But such changes would be very expensive at this stage in the process, the builder explained, promising that, "When the house is done, you'll love it." However, the house didn't get better, and when it was finished, it was clear to both of them that they felt no affinity for it. It seemed ostentatious to them. The scale of each room was overwhelming.

Laura took me upstairs to show me the master bathroom. "Look at this," she exclaimed, "our previous bedroom wasn't even this size!" Although the couple now faulted themselves

This soaring living room was designed to impress, not to be a comfortable space for the activities of daily life.

for being naive, they were simply following the process that is standard to working with a builder and selecting from a stock set of plans. They were not offered an opportunity for input into the design. And they didn't know how to ask for or give the feedback necessary to make it an expression of their lifestyle and their values. Like many people building a new house, Paul and Laura didn't have the words to describe what they wanted, nor did they realize how important it was to have input into the "feel" of the house. If a builder hears that a home buyer wants a spacious family room, he reasonably assumes that they are asking for a BIG family room. To Paul and Laura,

almost anything would have seemed spacious compared to their previous home.

The outcome was that Paul and Laura had built a $500,000 house that was nowhere close to their dream of home. After spending almost three times the value of their previous house, they were deeply unhappy. They told me they felt no desire to make the house their own by furnishing it or personalizing it in any way. Their story was horrifying to me. And even more alarming is the fact that Paul and Laura are not alone. Over the last couple of years, more and more people who have lived in these impersonal, oversized houses have come to our office and asked, "Is there an alternative? Can you design us a house that is more beautiful and more reflective of our personalities—a house we will enjoy living in?"

The answer is, of course, yes. And the key lies in building Not So Big, in spending more money on the quality of the space and less on the sheer quantity of it. So this book is for Paul and Laura and for everyone like them, whether building from scratch or remodeling, who wants a special home that expresses something significant about their lives and values but who doesn't know how to get it.

The Case for Comfort

After designing homes for 15 years, I have come to an inevitable conclusion: We are all searching for home, but we are trying to find it by building more rooms and more space. Instead of thinking about the quality of the spaces we live in, we tend to focus on quantity. But a house is so much more than its size and volume, neither of which has anything to do with comfort.

Instead of quantity,
think quality.
Comfort is born of
smaller scale and
beautiful details.

11

Everything in this kitchen conspires to create a classic statement, from custom cabinetry to antique light fixtures.

When most people contemplate building a new house or remodeling an existing one, they tend to spend time focusing on floorplan options and square footage. But in a completed home, these are only a very small part of what makes an impression. What also defines the character of a house are the details, such as a beautiful stair railing, well-crafted moldings around windows and doors, and useful, finely tailored built-ins.

These details are what attract us to older homes. New homes should be no different. However, such details cost money. And unless people are working with an architect, it is unusual to spend much time thinking about these aspects of the design. Because most people start with a desire for more space than their budgets allow, anything more than basic space, minimally detailed, will exceed the budget.

It's the details that delight: An Arts and Crafts–inspired light fixture can make a bigger impression than a vaulted ceiling.

Natural light and a stained-glass window beautify a stair landing. In a Not So Big House, every space is considered to be an expression of the lives lived within.

People who are attracted to architecturally designed houses also tend to seek a higher level of detail. So a good architect will suggest reducing square footage to allow for more detail. It isn't unusual for an architect's estimate of square-foot cost to be half again as much as a builder's. The architect is simply aware that, given the client's desire for detail, a house without detail is not going to be satisfactory. We're already familiar with this design concept in automobiles. The quality and detail of a Mercedes, Lexus, or Jaguar are far more important than the size of the car. More space does not equal more comfort. In fact, size has nothing to do with the appeal of these cars. If you want nothing but space, you buy an equally expensive diesel truck.

I do not advocate that everyone live in small houses. What I do suggest is that when building a new home or remodeling an existing one, you evaluate what really makes you feel at home. In other words, concentrate on, and put more of your money toward, what you like rather than settling for sheer size and volume. This concept is just as applicable to someone building a very expensive home as it is to someone on a tight

The Not So Big House of the Past

Around the turn of the last century, two Englishmen warned that the machine age could very well destroy the quality of life. John Ruskin and William Morris believed that life needed to be rehumanized, and the first place to begin such an undertaking was in the home. Ruskin and Morris founded a movement that was called Arts and Crafts, and it encompassed everything from the design of textiles to the design of houses.

Our neighborhoods are filled with examples of Not So Big Houses from the past, like the Craftsman bungalow above.

The Arts and Crafts home was custom-crafted and featured large fireplaces and built-in bookshelves and cabinets. In North America, the style was embraced by such architects and designers as Greene and Greene and Gustav Stickley. Other American architects, among them Frank Lloyd Wright, created styles that were also based on notions of craft and beauty. For those Americans who couldn't afford an architect-designed home, Sears sold a prebuilt bungalow—complete with built-in shelves, wood trim, and a front porch—which arrived in panels and was easily as-

An Arts and Crafts interior designed by Greene and Greene (right).

sembled. (In 1926, a two-bedroom bungalow was listed in the Sears catalogue for the affordable price of $626.)

Smaller houses still seem connected to a simpler time. Many of the older houses in our neighborhoods were built to offer solace in a changing world. Now, nearly 100 years later, we seem to have forgotten the ideas Ruskin and Morris were so passionate about. Houses are getting bigger and bigger, and, because square footage is all that is required, they are being built without the level of detail so important to humanizing life.

This room was designed to be a total expression of comfort, exemplified by the cozy scale, built-ins, and arched ceiling.

budget. While you might be able to afford a 6,000-sq.-ft. house, you may find that building a 3,000-sq.-ft. house that fits your lifestyle actually gives you more space to *live* in. In most very large homes, a substantial percentage of space is rarely used. And if you have a limited budget, this book will give you ideas on how to pare down the quantity of space you need so that you can put more of your money into giving the house some character.

Creating Comfort

The current pattern of building big to allow for quantities of furniture with still more room to spare is more akin to wearing a sack than a tailored suit. It may offer capacity, but at the cost of comfort and charm. Spaciousness, although it can look appealing in a photograph, just isn't conducive to comfort. Many of the huge rooms we see in magazines today are really only comfortable to be in when they are filled with people. For

No other space in a house says "comfort" quite like a window seat. Sitting here feels like an embrace from the house.

one or two, or for a family, they can be overwhelming. And when rooms feel overwhelming, they don't get used.

The Not So Big House, no matter its style, aims to be comfortable. Look up the word "comfortable" in any dictionary and you'll see a range of entries attempting to describe it. Webster's offers a wide variety of definitions, from "fitted to give tranquil enjoyment" to "free from pain and trouble." So how do we create comfort in the Not So Big House?

One of the tools that can help you determine what feels comfortable is to gain a better understanding of the proportions of space. Like most people, Paul and Laura were not able to understand from the blueprints what the space would feel like. Proportion literally refers to the relationship of the vertical to the horizontal dimension. It also includes the relationship to the third dimension, depth. Because we are human beings and come in sizes typically ranging from just under 5 ft.

to mid-6 ft., those three dimensions also need to relate to our human height. Some people can just tell when a space is pleasingly proportioned, while other people cannot. The ability to read a space this way is similar to an "ear" for music.

But not everyone agrees on what is well-proportioned space. Many people find Frank Lloyd Wright's much-acclaimed work to be oppressive, either because they consider it to be too ordered or because it's too constrictive for head height in some places. Wright used low ceilings to accentuate transitions between various significant places in the house, as well as at entryways, to give one the sense of needing to stoop, which is a gesture of reverence. On the other hand, the Prairie Style (the name his architectural style has come to be known by) liberated a new way of thinking about space and proportion in

Architect Frank Lloyd Wright was a master of proportion. He used variations in ceiling height to enhance character and comfort in his homes.

architectural design. For many people, the variations in ceiling height typical of his work greatly enhance the character and comfort of a home (see the bottom photo on the facing page).

Consider the foyer in Paul and Laura's suburban house. Why was it so unwelcoming? Well, with its tall ceilings and marble floors, it was designed to overwhelm and impress visitors, not to welcome. The proportions of their foyer were more suitable for a public building than for a house. When a space is overscaled, in relation to our own size, more often than not it doesn't feel comfortable.

The book *A Pattern Language* (Oxford University Press, 1977) has been a very useful tool in our office. Written by Christopher Alexander and a group of colleagues, the book consists of a collection of concepts, or patterns, that range from issues of city planning to those of individual room configuration. We use the book to help clients think about and describe how they want to tailor their house to their lifestyle and how to make it comfortable. One of my favorite patterns described in the book is entitled "Alcoves." It states that, "No homogeneous room, of homogeneous height, can serve a group of people well. To give a group a chance to be together, as a group, a room must also give them the chance to be alone, in ones and twos in the same space." It concludes, "Therefore…make small places at the edge of any common room usually no more than 6 feet wide and 3 to 6 feet deep and possibly much smaller. These alcoves should be large enough for two people to sit, chat or plan and sometimes large enough to contain a desk or a table."

What the pattern describes perfectly is how to make a space comfortable. By dividing a room into smaller spaces, it can be

A window seat is tucked into the second floor, allowing a cozy place for one within a house designed for entertaining.

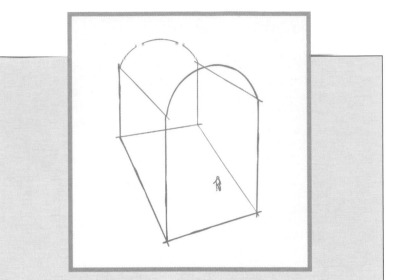

Finding Comfort

When I teach design, I ask first-year architecture students to collect data about places that make them feel particularly comfortable or uncomfortable. This is also a useful exercise for non-architects who want to understand better how the places that surround us affect us.

A big space, however inspiring, can be too tall for comfort.

Here's how it works. Equip yourself with a tape measure and a pad of paper. As you go about your daily routine, notice how you respond to different places—whether the place is as splendid as the rotunda in the State Capitol or as mundane as the copy room at the office. In each place you visit, notice how you respond. When I walk through the magnificent doorway at the State Capitol here in Minnesota, I feel awe and wonder. Physically, though, I feel very small, almost insignificant in this towering space, despite the beauty of the surroundings.

In smaller spaces, it's useful to measure the proportions of the room—and don't forget the ceiling height. As you measure, notice what constitutes the spaces that feel good to you. Try to determine if they appeal on an emotional level or in a physical way. And try to articulate why. Such spaces are the shapes that make you feel most comfortable and are worth incorporating in your own home.

used for a variety of functions while offering human-scaled spaces that are actually connected to things that go on in the house. I call this idea "shelter around activity," and one of the best examples of it is the window seat. The floor is raised, the ceiling is lowered and the walls are brought in to define a place for one or two people, from which they can observe the world. Sitting in a window seat feels like an embrace from the house. It is the epitome of comfort.

I designed a house for a single woman who loved to entertain. While many of the spaces in her house were suitable for large numbers of people, I wanted to make sure that the house had some places that would be comfortable when she was alone. Her window seat on the second floor is tucked into the geometry of the roofline (see the photo on p. 17), which offers shelter around activity and a bird's-eye view of the nearby lake.

One of my partners, Michaela Mahady, designed the living room shown in the photo on p. 15 to be a total expression of comfort. Not only does the fieldstone hearth bespeak comfort, but the small scale of the room also ensures coziness. The arch above the fireplace, the lowered soffits at the edge of the room, the soft lighting, the abundance of natural woodwork, even the overstuffed furniture—everything conspires to make this room one you want to spend time in.

Tailoring to Fit

Paul and Laura had embarked on a new house project because they needed a place for their boys to play indoors during the winter. But despite its size and cost, the house they had built still didn't offer this space. The would-be living room projected such a formality, because of its scale, that the whole family

In a house where every detail expresses the personality of its owners, a rope and a tree trunk become a stair railing and a load-bearing column.

The wooden railing features cut-out fish and trees, which express the family's favorite pastime and the house's North Woods location.

shared one main living space—the kitchen/family room. If their needs had been given more careful analysis before construction, a very different solution would have evolved.

As my meeting with Paul and Laura continued they told me that their lack of desire to personalize their new home came from the fact that it communicated nothing at all about who

they were—to themselves or to the community. In fact, the house projected an image that they found fundamentally offensive. To them the house said "generic house of wealthy people," which wasn't at all how they saw themselves.

Clearly, what should happen before a house is planned or built is an analysis of the lives—the likes, dislikes, needs, and wishes—of the people who will live in it. Just as a tailor takes measurements before sewing a new suit, we should take measurements before building a new house. There are few things in life as personal as our homes. Personalizing a home, though, goes beyond decoration. Because it takes considerable thought and planning to make a house into a home, I advocate far greater participation in the design process by the people who will live in the house. Your house should be an expression of who you are, not something that's impersonal and generic.

A stair railing can be just a safety barrier, but if it's designed with the homeowner in mind, it can become a centerpiece for the house. In the examples shown here and on the previous page, the railings were custom-crafted to express something about the people who live there. The rope railing in the photo on p. 19, designed by an architect couple, came as a solution only after 10 other ideas had been abandoned. The husband, an avid sailor, loved the idea of the rope, which also works in a similar way to the organic form of the tree-trunk column. Both rope and tree serve a function, as well as imbue the house with personality. The photo at left shows a cabin on a North Woods island that was built as a weekend retreat for a family that loves to fish. The stair railing, inspired by the work of the Scandinavian artist Carl Larsson, illustrates both the woodsy location of the cabin and the family's favorite hobby.

In this remodeled house, a favorite window was saved and reused in an addition, where it is now flanked with glass block and double-hung windows.

Windows can be custom-tailored to frame a special view or to make a striking interior statement. In the remodeled house shown in the photo above, the couple's favorite window was saved from the original house and moved out 8 ft. to the new face of the home. A glass-block transom and flanking double-hung windows were added to let in more of the south light. Circular windows are expensive, but they can also become a focal point for the entire house. In the house shown on p. 22, an 8-ft.-diameter circular window frames a spectacular view while also creating an equally splendid interior focal point that's visible from many parts of the house. A circular effect can be achieved less expensively, but with equal drama, by hanging a metal hoop inside a perfectly square picture window (see the photo on p. 23).

A circular window can frame spectacular views and become the focal point of an interior space.

A circular effect can be achieved inexpensively by inserting a metal hoop into a square window.

Often a work of art or a special piece of furniture has particular meaning, and a house can be designed to accommodate such objects. The carved wooden owl shown in the top photo on p. 24 became a symbol of the owners' land, which was frequently visited by an owl, and of their first house, which had burned to the ground. When they designed their new home, the wooden owl, a survivor of the fire, was offered a special place by the front entrance, where it greets all who enter.

Another couple, who had collected art and furniture for most of their adult lives, wanted a retirement house that would be a backdrop for their collection (see the bottom photo on p. 24). So the wall in the dining area was recessed to create a niche just the right size for a special Japanese *tansu*, or storage chest. The painting over the buffet has its own display area, which was anticipated in the design process. White walls throughout the house provide a dramatic setting for the collection.

Houses are repositories of the things that have meaning to us. In this Prairie-influenced home, a carved wooden owl greets visitors from its built-in niche.

This contemporary interior was designed to showcase a collection of paintings and furniture, with a niche designed specifically for a Japanese *tansu*.

The garden shed shown in the photo on the facing page is modeled after a Wendy house, or an English child's playhouse inspired by the Peter Pan stories. In the process of remodeling a couple's Cape Cod home, Dale Mulfinger, one of my partners, discovered that the woman, an avid gardener, wanted a place to house her tools that would fit in stylistically with the house. Because gardening was her passion, Dale determined in the planning process to design for her a special place, rather than simply expanding the garage.

Tailoring is a basic ingredient of the Not So Big House. If you just make a house smaller, but still generic, it won't have any more appeal than its larger cousins. What makes the Not So

A tool shed designed for an avid gardener becomes a charming little house that matches the Cape Cod styling of the owner's home.

Keeping a Place Journal

In a three-ring binder, start to assemble data about the places in your life that make you feel comfortable and those that make you feel uncomfortable. Document their size, take photos, or make diagrams illustrating what it is within the space that evokes the response. Images of other spaces can supplement your notes—magazines are a great resource for this. Some current favorites for gathering images are: *Architectural Digest, Better Homes and Gardens Building Ideas, Better Homes and Gardens Home Plan Ideas, Better Homes and Gardens Remodeling Ideas, Elle Decor, Fine Homebuilding, Fine Homebuilding's annual Houses issue, Home Magazine, House and Garden, House Beautiful Home Building, Metropolitan Home,* and *Traditional Home.*

Big concept work is that superfluous square footage is traded for less tangible but more meaningful aspects of design that are about beauty, self-expression, and the enhancement of life.

Working with Paul and Laura, we started to identify what features they wanted in a home. These included window seats, a place for the adults to retreat to after dinner while the kids play in the family room, lots of built-ins and bookshelves, and a large amount of natural woodwork. In contrast to the 4,000-sq.-ft. house they are currently living in, their new house will be around 2,300 sq. ft. Despite its smaller size, it will cost only slightly less to build. This is because for this couple, quality and personality are important. And now they understand that that is where their money needs to go. No matter how big or how small you make it, a house will not be a home unless you, your architect, and your builder really craft it into a place that is tailored to the way you live, filled with the spaces and things that have meaning to you.

Cotswold cottages in England built from stone have lasted hundreds of years.

Built to Last

When I first started designing houses in the early 1980s, many of our clients were asking for help in making their homes energy efficient. When the tax credit for such strategies disappeared, most of the interest in energy efficiency left with it. At that point, my partners and I realized that if the homes we designed were to be energy efficient, it would be because we wanted them to be, not because our clients were requesting it. Like many other architects and builders, we continued to design houses that would minimize a reliance on fossil fuels. We also insist upon good construction practices, even though it is a rare client who asks for a house that will last for generations.

America is a country of pioneers. And, as Americans, we assume that the way to embody our dreams in a house is to build it new for ourselves. It's the exception rather than the rule for people to stay where they are planted. People don't assume that they will pass their home on to the next generation, so building for permanence has never held much appeal or value. But, gradually, this attitude is changing. Why do we love Europe so much? Because of a sense of history, which is told best by buildings built centuries ago and made to last.

Along with this dawning appreciation for building for the long term comes the recognition that we will take care of things that are beautiful. Beauty, more often than not, comes from careful crafting. And when a well-crafted object ages, no matter what it is, society almost always helps it to age well. Just look at the buildings our culture has chosen to preserve—all of them were well designed. Owner after owner of such homes has recognized the treasure inherited and cared for them lovingly.

Fallingwater, Frank Lloyd Wright's masterpiece, is an important part of America's cultural heritage. Its beauty inspires us to take care of the building, ensuring that it will stand for future generations.

The Not So Big House is built for the future by taking care of the present. Anyone who has driven past a construction site and seen the dumpsters filled with perfectly good building materials understands that there must be a better way. By building the Not So Big House with materials that are renewable and by limiting the expenditure to what will really make a difference to the quality of life, we can have an enormous impact on our lives today as well as on the future.

What I am proposing in this book is that our houses can express our personalities, that they can be designed to accommodate our changing lifestyles, and that they can be built for future generations.

"When shown into one of those polar parlors...the heart cries, 'Take me where the people stay; I didn't come to see the chairs.'"
—William C. Gannett

For a residential architect, going to a party in a new house is like test-driving a new car—it's a chance to see how the house works under real-world conditions. When my husband and I recently attended the wedding reception of an old college friend, we were among 40 guests at the hosts' first big party in their new suburban home. The house was outfitted with all the trappings of a dream home—an impressive front foyer, an elegant living room, and a formal dining room. It seemed the perfect place for a wedding reception. If ever there were an occasion when the formal rooms of a house would be well used, this was it.

The reality was quite different, however—yet strangely predictable. During the entire party, the living room remained vacant except for the occasional guest who walked through to admire the art as if viewing pictures in a museum. Even the dining room, which was filled with a splendid display of food, was empty. Where was everybody? Crowded into the kitchen, where they were leaning on

every possible surface; or in the well-used family room, which had an assortment of comfortable furniture.

Every half hour or so the hostess would try to coax people out of the kitchen by calling out, "The food is in the dining room!" Whenever someone actually ventured into the dining room and returned with a plate of food, invariably there was a chorus of, "Where did you get that?"

Even though the family room and the kitchen are the most popular places in a home, many houses still feature beautifully appointed formal living and dining rooms that sit empty most of the time, awaiting the arrival of guests. Although life at the end of the 20th century is quite informal, Emily Post still rules over the floorplans of our houses, making sure that they mind their manners.

In most houses, the formal rooms for dining and living are dinosaurs—leftovers from the turn of the century when Victorian house design followed the social code of the day. Visitors were ushered into a formal parlor. Dinner was served in a formal dining room, typically located a circuitous distance from the kitchen. Children were seen and not heard. One hundred years later, these formal areas still define

Partygoers often assemble in the kitchen and family room, even when you don't want them to.

Living rooms are built for parties, yet during this gathering the room remained completely empty.

the house. It's as if visitors are presented with a stage set, while the people who live there spend their time backstage. We've put all the resources necessary into creation of the living room for our guests while we do without new carpeting in the family room. The front door is used twice a year, usually for parties, and the people who live in the house enter through the back door, past piles of dirty laundry and bags of bottles ready for recycling. The irony is that, even when guests do come over, they avoid the formal spaces created for them because they're *too* formal.

Yet we continue to live informally in houses designed for more formality. Since World War II, there's been an attempt to incorporate more informal places into our houses. Remember the den? The basement rec room? How about the wet bar, the party room, the pool room? Many 1970s suburban homes offered one or more of the assortment, but the formal living and dining rooms are still at the core of the footprint of a house. And beginning in the 1980s, a vast variety of rooms joined the roster of must-have spaces, including great rooms, entertainment rooms, lavish master suites, and spaces for the newfound fitness craze.

Rethink your house and you'll discover the places that are used everyday—this is the essence of the Not So Big House.

Essentially, however, today's houses still wear the architectural equivalent of a hoopskirt, even if the accessories seem more contemporary. While we've been busy evolving over the past century, most of our houses have not. Their evolution has been constricted by outdated notions of what we think we need and what the real estate industry says we need for resale. At the turn of the new century, most houses are designed for the turn of the last.

It's time to rethink our houses and to let them become expressions of the way we really live. A Not So Big House can be Not So Big because the "dinosaur" rooms are replaced with spaces that reflect the way we eat and the way we live. The floorplan of the Not So Big House is a map, not a fossil, that reveals the lives of the people who live in it today.

Formal living rooms are rarely used in most houses; they stand almost as a memorial to the way we used to live.

Rethinking the Room

When I was 10 years old, my elementary school teacher assigned the class a puzzle, which she wanted us to solve by thinking creatively. The solution offers the essence of how to think about design. Here's the problem: Without taking pen off paper, and using only four straight lines, connect the nine dots shown at the top of the facing page. At home I spent hours on the problem and grew increasingly frustrated. I knew my teacher wouldn't lie to us, that there must be an answer. Yet it appeared to be an impossible assignment. During the middle of the night, however, I awoke with the answer clear in my mind.

I reached for the problem and magically connected the dots with four straight lines. What I discovered was that, if I stayed within the box created by the dots, I couldn't solve the problem. Once I broke the confines of the outline, the problem solved itself. (If you have trouble solving the problem, you'll find the answer on the very last page of the book—but don't give up yet.)

Is there a way to think beyond ordinary boundaries to create a house that works better for us? This is the secret to designing a Not So Big House—the ability to think creatively, responding to needs and wishes, not to preconceived notions of what a house should be.

Instead of thinking of a house as a series of rooms, think of it as a sequence of places. One favorite place is a cozy spot by the hearth.

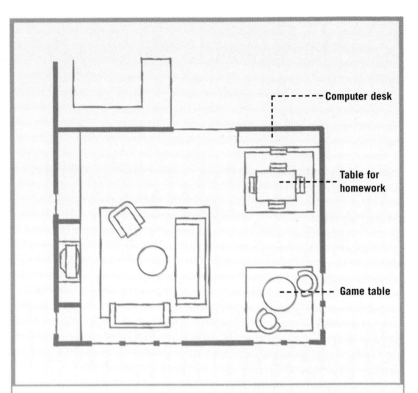

Computer desk

Table for homework

Game table

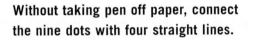

Without taking pen off paper, connect the nine dots with four straight lines.

Saving Space with Alcoves

One space can accommodate three different activity places (above), each gravitating toward a corner. House the same activities in alcoves (below) and you reduce the square footage and use the space more efficiently.

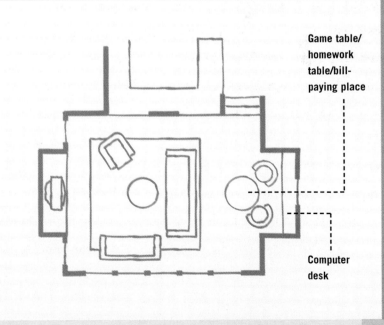

Game table/ homework table/bill-paying place

Computer desk

Most people speak in terms of square footage and number of rooms when asked to describe a house: four bedrooms, three baths, 3,000 sq. ft. The idea that a house is composed of rooms for separate activities is fundamental to how it's been defined. But a room is an artificial construct, an attempt to put boundaries around space. The idea of the room can be replaced with the notion of places for various activities. What is your favorite place in your home? Is it a comfortable chair near the fireplace where you can enjoy a glass of wine and unwind after a day of work? Mine is a little book nook, a place just big enough for one that's carved into a corner of the living area. This place offers a cozy spot to read and a place to watch what's going on in the rest of the house.

In a Not So Big House, each space is defined by the activities that take place there. Think about what happens in the family room: There's a place to watch TV, a place to enjoy the

Understanding Where You Live Now

Take a look at your existing home. Now make a list of the rooms you have, along with the approximate square footage of each one. Under each room name, list what happens there. Under each activity, list the frequency of the activity and who does it. Finally, reorganize the list of rooms in order of most used to least used.

For most people, this exercise offers some surprises. A room that has significant square footage may not be used very often. This is a clear indication that you should rethink the space to see if there's another way to accommodate the activities it houses. In many cases, rooms such as the formal living room and formal dining room serve limited purposes.

Some people will discover that the formal living room is in use every day. In that case, the living room works. The point is to identify how you live and then tailor the house to accommodate those needs rather than just assume that every house has to have the same set of rooms.

fireplace, a place to do homework, a place to pay bills, a place to play Scrabble. When we think of the family room in this way, it's no longer merely a space bounded by four walls and a ceiling. It can be defined another way altogether: as a series of alcoves, each offering shelter around an activity and surrounding a central sitting area (see the drawing on p. 33 and the photo on the facing page). When this kind of thinking is extended to the entire house, a new definition emerges. A house is a sequence of places for all the different activities that happen there.

One reason houses have become too big is that they are planned with the idea that there needs to be a separate room for each activity. But look carefully at how you really live in your house and you'll discover how much space goes unused (see the sidebar at left). A house is Not So Big when it's composed of adaptable spaces, each designed to share various functions, each in use everyday.

Exercise: Understanding Where You Live Now

Kitchen 8×12 = 96 SF
Cooking
Making coffee
Eating breakfast & snacks
Reading paper

Dining Room 10×12 = 120 SF
Eating dinner
Entertaining (4-5 times per year)

Living Room 14×16 = 224 SF
Entertaining (4-5 times per year)
Reading
Listening to music

Foyer 5×10 = 50 SF
Coming & going in the non-winter months
Hanging coats
Greeting guests

Laundry 7×10 = 70 SF
Washing clothes
Hanging dry & drying clothes
Filing newspaper clippings

Bathroom 7×8 = 56 SF
The obvious - only one bathroom so it all happens here

Bedroom #1 10×10 = 100 SF
Kid's sleeping place
Storage of off-season clothing

Bedroom #2 12×13 = 156 SF
Our bedroom
Reading in evening

Bedroom #3 9×13 = 117 SF
Storage of books - so it's really a library
More storage of off-season clothes
Other crafts

Attic 10×24 = 240 SF
In home office space
Paying bills
Drawing
Designing
Internet access from computer here
Watching TV
Listening to music
Meditating
Reading
Also serves as extra bedroom when we have guests

MOST TO LEAST USED
1. Kitchen   96
2. Attic   240
3. Bathroom   56
4. Foyer   50
5. Bedroom #2   156
6. Laundry   70
7. Dining Room   120
8. Bedroom #3   117
9. Living Room   224
10. Bedroom #1

The Not So Big House features adaptable spaces open to one another, designed for everyday use.

If you rethink the formal living room, formal dining room, kitchen, and family room, you'll discover a different model altogether, not unlike the way the nine dots are connected in the exercise mentioned previously. The core of the Not So Big House is an interconnected area that encompasses kitchen, living, and dining functions. All of these areas, which are physically and visibly open to each other, are shared by family and friends.

A balance between public and private space is essential to making any floorplan work. In this house, private spaces for adults are balanced by open areas for family activities. (Photo taken at A on floorplan p. 38.)

Public and Private Spaces

A realtor who had recently purchased a striking contemporary remodel of an older home called me with an odd complaint. Ever since she and her husband had moved into the house they had been fighting. An architect is typically not a marriage counselor, but I agreed to take a look. The house, with its white walls, high ceilings, and contemporary feel (see the photo at right), was ready for the pages of *Architectural Digest.* But as my tour progressed, the couple's problem became clear. There wasn't a single door inside the house, not even on the bathroom, which very stylishly featured a soaring arch to mark its entrance. The master bedroom had a half-wall that looked over into the living room. There was no privacy in this house for anybody, which clearly was creating tension between husband and wife.

The remodeling was fairly straightforward. Rather than build walls, we extended the half-walls with glass to provide acoustic privacy and to preserve the striking lines of the design. As for the bathroom, we added a door and filled the archway with a window that still allowed light to stream in.

Another client, living alone in a brand-new 5,000-sq.-ft. house, called me because she wanted to plan an addition.

When there are no doors to separate one space from another, a house offers no privacy.

When we met she confided that the house, believe it or not, felt too small to her—and she was right! In spite of its high square footage, the house was incredibly claustrophobic. There were countless rooms, each designated for a specific activity, and equally countless doorways that, when open, offered dead-end views of walls. There was nothing to look at beyond each room, no view of any other interior spaces—and deliberately so. In planning the house, the woman, who considered herself to be a terrible housekeeper, had wanted to make sure that her guests could not see into any of her messy rooms. She hadn't recognized that her need to add on was a direct result of this strategy.

Rather than add on, we reconfigured part of the existing space by opening up the maze of rooms into an open, public space. We kept the balance of rooms intact. As for the housekeeping issue, I gently suggested that she consider hiring some cleaning help.

To make any floorplan work, there has to be a balance between open spaces and closed, between public and private. Sometimes we feel like being with others, and other times we need solitude. A house should offer a hierarchy of spaces, each appropriate to its function and to our mood. The Not So Big House has at its core a public space

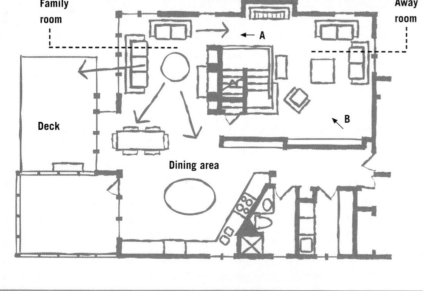

Family room

Away room

Deck

A sitting area down the hall provides a private place for adults—in the Not So Big floorplan it's called the "away room." (Photo taken at B on floorplan.)

The plan shows how an informal living area can become the central part of the house when it's visible from many places.

Dining area

composed of living, dining, and kitchen functions. It also allows for private spaces, which are acoustically or visually separate from the open areas.

One of my partners designed a house for a professional couple who wanted spaces for the family to gather together, as well as places for adults only. The light-filled living area shown in the photo on p. 36 is the most public space in the house because it's visible from the kitchen, from a more secluded sitting area, from a second-floor loft, and from an exterior deck (see the floorplan on the facing page). When the adults need privacy, they retreat to the sitting area just down the hall (see the photo on the facing page).

How public or private a space is depends on both its scale and its visibility. If a place is to be used, people need to be able to see it. A space that's visible from as many places as possible automatically becomes a public area. If a space is to be private, remove it from sight and locate it away from the main traffic areas—or put a door at its entrance. "Out of sight, out of mind," is a truth in house design.

When there is a proper balance between public and private places, something quite natural happens. All the spaces in the house begin to be used every day. The patterns of life are no longer constrained by the floorplan; they are expressed by it.

The Public Kitchen

Back when cooking was a private act, the kitchen was concealed behind doors, anterooms, and walk-through butler's pantries. In the Victorian era, the kitchen was so private that most family members never even set foot inside it—it was entirely the territory of servants. Later in the century, however, the woman of the house took over the kitchen, emerging from its confines only after taking off her apron and wiping the sweat from her brow. But today, we love to be in the kitchen, and no matter how tiny the space, this is where friends and family congregate.

The kitchen is the heart of the house, and the Not So Big House should have a big heart. If we acknowledge that the kitchen is where we want to be, then we should make the kitchen accessible and open to all the living areas of the house. Extend the kitchen so that it's visible from the areas where you live; once it is connected—physically and visually—to these spaces, then suddenly the need for a separate family room, sun-

Traditional Kitchen Placement

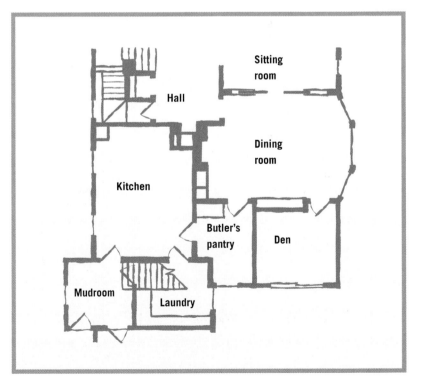

A hearth in the kitchen can offer a comfortable place for one or two people to sit, out of the way of food preparation but close to the center of activity.

room, and living room is gone. All that's necessary is a place for living, where family and visitors can gather near the kitchen.

You can even go so far as to offer a place to sit in the kitchen, by adding a hearth and a small cozy area where a few people can gather out of the traffic pattern of food preparation (see the photo on the facing page). This kind of space appeals to even the most citified folks, who long for the look and feel of the farmhouse kitchen. The image of this place, where bread bakes in an open hearth and sunlight streams in the windows, has captured our imaginations. The scale of this area is important to its success. It should be big enough for only a couple of easy chairs—the addition of just a few unnecessary feet destroys its coziness.

Double-Duty Dining

When a house is defined as a series of places for various activities rather than as a string of separate rooms, it's easy to see how often functions are duplicated in a typical floorplan. Many newer houses, for example, offer two or three rooms in which to eat. The first and most prominent is the formal dining room, which is usually a room set apart from the kitchen and main living areas. There is also an informal eating area, adjacent to the kitchen or a part of it. And sometimes there's a still more informal eating place at the kitchen island, where stools are pulled up to the countertop surface (see the floorplan on p. 42).

The dining room is not as universally neglected as the formal living room, but in many homes it is used only once or twice a year. Rather than put your resources into a room used so infrequently, why not create a place for dining that can do double duty—for everyday use, as well as for those few formal

The kitchen is the heart of the Not So Big House; connected to the living and dining areas, it's a gathering place for family and friends.

The Integrated Kitchen

Kitchen design has reached new heights of sophistication. But while a kitchen may boast the latest equipment and appliances, most kitchens still look fairly generic. When the kitchen is open to the rest of the house, the opportunity exists to integrate it visually. If a house features natural woodwork in its public areas, then the kitchen should feature natural woodwork as well. If a house makes a stark contemporary statement, so should the kitchen.

In simple terms, the materials that are used in the rest of the house are brought into the kitchen. Rather than use generic kitchen cabinetry, tie the kitchen together with the rest of the living area by installing custom cabinets. If you have a tile floor in the front entryway, consider running tiles as a backsplash along the counters. Choose carefully which kitchen gadgets are left out and which are stored. A hanging rack of well-designed implements, carefully placed, can become part of the kitchen's composition.

If you are using a center island, consider it as you would a built-in piece of furniture. The flooring materials used can also connect the kitchen with the living and dining spaces. Countertops, too, can make a striking statement. There are many resources to help you make your kitchen work exactly the way you want it to: As you plan for its usefulness, think also about its beauty.

Tiles used in the front entryway can be repeated as a backsplash along the counters.

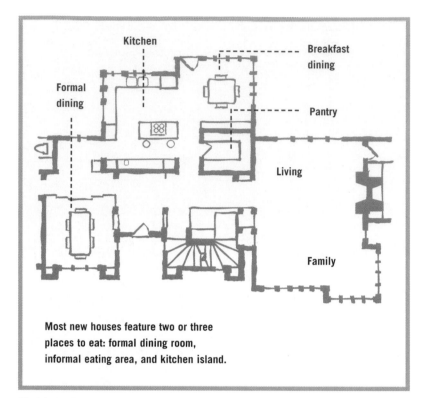

Most new houses feature two or three places to eat: formal dining room, informal eating area, and kitchen island.

Multiple Dining Areas

occasions? Just as a living area can work for both family and friends, so can one dining area function both for family snacks and for a dinner party. The top photo on p. 44 illustrates the key to making a place for eating work both formally and informally. The eating area was designed to accommodate a long table, which seats 6 informally and up to 12 or more on more special occasions with the addition of table leaves. Combining the informal and formal eating areas into one saves at least 200 sq. ft.

But what about the dirty dishes? Many cooks are concerned about guests seeing their messy kitchens. There are various solutions to hiding the detritus of meal preparation. A raised countertop between kitchen and dining area will obstruct the

Everyone loves to be in the kitchen, and the Not So Big House puts dining close to the place of food preparation.

view of the mess (as shown in the photo below). The sink and the dishwasher can be placed so they aren't in full view from the table. Or a series of sliding panels, illustrated on the facing page, can totally hide the kitchen.

If you enjoy the experience of creating a special atmosphere in a dining room that's separated from the kitchen—and don't want to give it up just to save a few hundred square feet—then this option isn't for you. However, remember that just because the dining area is informal in layout doesn't mean it will feel informal to your guests. An informal eating area can easily become a more formal space with some simple lighting strategies, which are addressed in chapter 3 (see pp. 66-67).

A dining area can do double duty, serving equally well for everyday use and for formal occasions, with simple strategies like special lighting.

A raised countertop between kitchen and living area helps hide dirty dishes from view.

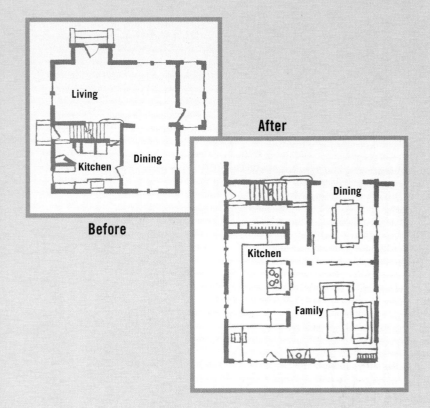

Before

After

A sliding partition between kitchen and dining room can be used to connect the areas or make them totally separate.

This type of partition is a good solution when remodeling an existing older home to fit more informal lifestyles.

Remodeling for Double-Duty Dining

The most common addition to an older house is a kitchen remodel with adjacent family room. This addition almost always includes an informal eating area. Once this new space exists, what were the formal living and dining room are rarely ever used again.

The floorplans shown here illustrate a way to avoid the atrophy of the dining room. Two of the walls in the old dining room were removed to open it to the new family-room addition. Visible from the kitchen and family area, the dining area can now do double-duty: both as the informal eating area for the family and for special occasions, when closing the sliding doors creates a more formal atmosphere.

An away room is a place for acoustical privacy. This away room is adjacent to the family room but separated by French doors. It offers a quiet space away from the noise of televisions and stereos. (Photo taken at A on floorplan.)

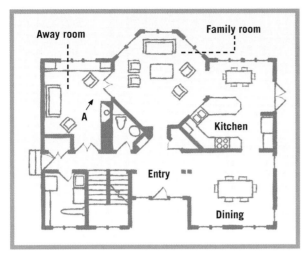

The Away Room

The "Away Room"

Imagine you drop by a neighbor's house for coffee. She ushers you inside her beautiful house, where one of the kids is watching an after-school special in the living area while another child is playing Nintendo. The teenager upstairs is listening to music—and it's not the harpsichord. Add the hum of a dishwasher to this cacophony, and you may wish you had never stopped by.

Because houses are filled with televisions, appliances, computers, and stereo equipment, they are filled with noise. In a more open floorplan, there needs to be a place that provides acoustical privacy. In our office we call this place the "away room," a term that refers to its function of providing escape (see the photo on the facing page). The away room can have several functions: It can be both the cozy and slightly more formal entertainment space where you can sit with other adults, and it can become a quiet place where adults can retreat to read or to work in the evenings.

In this house, the away room, smaller and less central than the classic formal living room, is the space for television viewing.

If the away room contains the television or the stereo, it becomes the place to watch or listen. Conversely, if the television or stereo is kept in the living area, the away room becomes the quiet area—a small, comfortable place away from the sound. Because the away room is separated from the more open living spaces by French doors or by distance, it can have a dif-

The everyday entrance to your house can be more than the back door—make it welcoming and beautiful. (Photos taken at A and B on floorplan.)

ferent style from the rest of the house. In a light and airy interior, the away room can be a cozy and book-lined alternative. If the house is filled with dark woodwork, then the away room can be filled with light.

The proportions of the room are important, as are its furnishings. A smaller scale—such as 11 ft. by 12 ft.—creates a cozier space. If the chairs are formal and uncomfortable, that's how you will feel. But if the away room is furnished with soft easy chairs, wicker rockers, and old family photos, it will offer a comfortable place for living.

The Entrance

The front door may be the most unused part of a house, especially in colder climates, opened only for visitors or for special deliveries. The everyday entrance to the house is usually through the back door. But why do we relegate ourselves to secondary status when it comes to the way we enter our houses?

Instead of thinking about the entry as just a front or back door, we can create a sequence of places and a more ceremonious greeting for ourselves than the passage from the garage, past the hot water heater, and through the laundry. Your everyday entrance should welcome you home. And that entrance

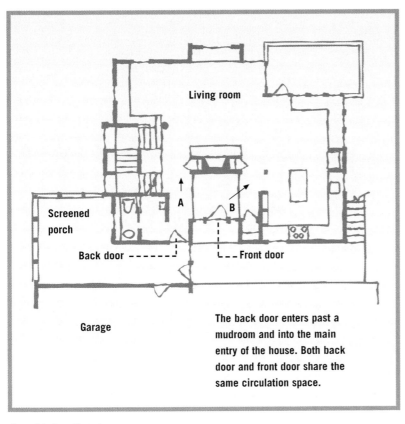

Living room

Screened
porch

Back door - - - - - - -

A

B

- - - Front door

Garage

The back door enters past a
mudroom and into the main
entry of the house. Both back
door and front door share the
same circulation space.

Combining Entries

can be combined with what has traditionally been called the front foyer to create a space that is actually used (see the photos on the facing page). By having two different doors opening into the same foyer—one a traditional front door and the other from a garage or adjacent mudroom—you and your visitors can enter the house more ceremoniously. In this model, the garage is placed close to the front entrance (see the floorplan above).

In many areas of the country, there needs to be a place where kids and adults can remove snowy or muddy shoes and coats. One solution is to attach the mudroom to the entry, either as an anteroom to a front foyer or just around the corner. Take off your outdoor clothing first, and then step into the entrance,

from which you are welcomed home by the views of your house. The point is to save square footage and to give residents a pleasant entry to their own home.

If the garage can't be close to the front door, it's a good idea for the entrance to open onto a space that offers a view to a window or to some special feature of the house. The stuff of everyday life that gets crammed into back hallways—the cat food, laundry, and piles of newspapers—can be placed in planned-for storage areas. They don't need to be the first things that greet you when you get home.

It can be difficult to combine formal and informal entries if the siting of the house dictates that the front entry be located away from the garage and back entry. And the necessary clean-up before entering the house may require a different model. The example that comes to mind is a farmer client whose wife insists he shower before he enters the house. Their mudroom is quite large, replete with laundry and full bath.

Home Work

In medieval times, the grocer, the bookbinder, and the cobbler, along with their help and their families, lived above their respective shops. It's only been in the last couple of hundred years that living has been separated from work space. But very recently—within the last decade even—work has begun to come back home. Our firm has designed numerous home offices, many of which were intended for evening use but have since developed into full-time work spaces. The challenge when incorporating a new function into your house is to go beyond merely adding square footage. How and when do you work? Who will interrupt you? How private does the space

French doors close off an office area from the master bedroom. This solution can offer the most private place to put a home office; in this instance, it allows a writer an escape from a young, active family.

need to be? What will your pattern of work be in the future? The examples illustrated here show five different approaches to integrating offices into the home.

Office attached to master bedroom A doctor who also writes books about health issues wanted to create a space within a 1926 Dutch Colonial where he could sit in a comfortable chair and read and also have a desk to work at his computer. He and his wife were facing the challenges of raising two active young children. It was determined that the most private place for the addition would be within the master bedroom suite. By adding no more than 80 sq. ft. to the master bedroom, we were able to create a distinctive reading nook and a workable office alcove (see the photo at right). The two sets of doors into the space—one into the master bedroom and then French doors that close off the office area—give him a kind of double-seal privacy.

Office in bedroom alcove A married couple contacted me about designing a weekend home. Because both of them were in professional positions, their weekend hideaway had to accommodate places to work. The woman, who is an attorney, didn't want her work space to be in the more public living area, so we carved a corner out of the master bedroom (see the top photo on p. 52). This nook, no wider than the desk itself, allows her

Through the French doors, the office area is actually an alcove tucked into the eaves of a low roofline. Many people would discard this area as unusable.

to study briefs while still enjoying the spectacular scenery. This option works well for people who are tidy—if your desk is usually cluttered you might consider an alcove that can be blocked from view with sliding doors.

Office in guest bedroom If you live in a house with a guest room, it can do double duty as an office. Putting an office in an infrequently used guest bedroom can be a good space-saving solution. The best way to double these two functions is to use a Murphy bed or a fold-out couch, so that the room doesn't stay filled with the bed platform. The size of this room should accommodate the bed both up and down. It's a good idea, however, to make sure there is at least 2 ft. 6 in. of clearance between the surrounding desk area and the bed. If the office computer is kept on a moveable cart, it can be rolled into another room during a guest's stay.

Office with separate entrance When my husband and I were designing our own home, we wanted a place with lots of counter space to lay out plans—and we knew that we needed a separate entrance in case clients came to the house. It also needed to be light-filled and pleasant to be in—if not, I knew we wouldn't use it. For us, the work space needed to be as interesting and as comfortable as the rest of the house.

The site we chose to build on is sloped, and the office, along with its separate entrance, occupies the lower level (see the photo below). The main living spaces are on the main and upper levels. The separate level for the office removes it enough from the living spaces so that we aren't constantly distracted by the lure of the refrigerator and other family activity.

Office for evening work A computer consultant needed an office that would be close to the activity of his family but that had enough separation to allow work to get done. The office was placed in the loop of family activity, so that when the doors are open, it can be part of the rest of the house (see the drawing on the facing page). If the doors are closed,

An alcove in the master bedroom, created by a lowered soffit, can easily become a home office—a solution that works well for tidy people.

The author's own home office is filled with light and is as interesting and as comfortable as the rest of the house.

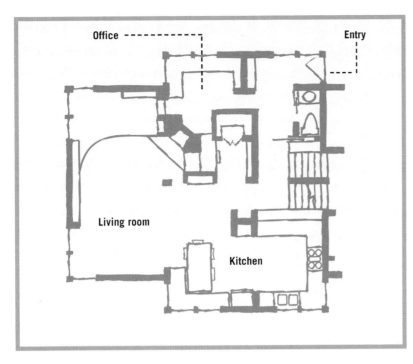

Home Office

though, he has acoustical privacy and his children know not to interrupt him. When a client comes to the house, he can close a door between the entry and living space, making the office entirely private.

If you're going to be doing a lot of work at home, it's better to create a space that is separate and private: Avoid making a home office double as the family control center. These are different functions and typically operate best out of different places.

Not So Many Bathrooms

The bathroom has undergone its own evolutionary process from water closet to luxury suite. American houses contain more bathrooms than any other culture's. Larger new homes feature one bathroom associated with each bedroom and sometimes even separate bathrooms for husband and wife. Add a

This bathroom serves both a master bedroom and a visiting child. Rather than build two separate bathrooms, resources were combined to make the bathroom as beautiful as possible. (Photo taken at A on floorplan.)

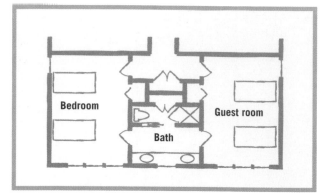

Bathroom with Two Entrances

Two doors into one bathroom (above) can create an awkward situation for visitors. One entrance into the same bathroom (left) is a better solution.

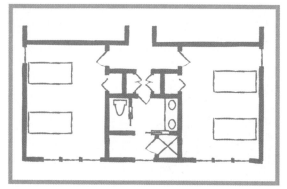

In designing a Not So Big House, there should be a concerted effort to cut back on the number of bathrooms. Here are a couple of strategies to accomplish that goal: Consider which bathrooms can be shared. The master bath is typically more an expression of fantasy than reality. With its whirlpool or soaking tub, the master bath implies a life of leisure and relaxation. The reality, in many families, is that the tub is used most often by children under the age of five. If you want to share your bathroom with your children, then plan accordingly. If you don't, then consider putting the soaking tub in a place where everyone can use it.

A common mistake is to connect a guest bedroom and another bedroom with one bathroom. This almost always creates an awkward situation for the guest, who may not be comfortable sharing a bathroom with whomever is on the other side of the door. In such cases, consider designing a bathroom with a single entrance, easily accessible from both bedrooms (see the drawings at left). And by placing partitions between functions you can accommodate the needs of more than one person without any awkwardness.

powder room and a mudroom toilet, and you can have two or three bathrooms per resident. Why so many? The reasons are primarily for resale value. A private bathroom is considered to be a desirable luxury. Yet, bathrooms are one of the most expensive areas in the house per square foot (you could almost purchase a new car for every bathroom you build), so it's important to analyze whether such an investment is sensible.

The way bathrooms are planned to be used and the way they actually are used are entirely different. The model in most instances seems to be one bathroom for the adults and one for the children. In some families the master bathroom is used by the whole family, because the morning is the time when the family gathers socially. In other models, the parents' area is a private zone.

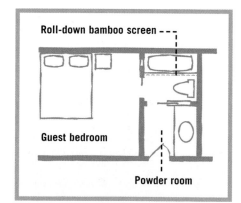

Powder Room/Guest Bathroom

A powder room should be convenient to family social areas and also close to the mudroom entrance. The same powder room can serve both family and visitors, if you're willing to let go of expectations that the room will be pristine at all times, ready for the arrival of an unannounced guest. Frequently when I tell clients this, they still insist they need two powder rooms: one for family and one for guests. But if you stop and think about how often a guest stops by unannounced, you'll be able to reevaluate whether it's worth building a separate powder room for such a rare event. That's how bathrooms proliferate—we don't think about how frequently such events (a guest arriving unannounced) really happen.

If a guest bedroom is nearby, the powder room can even function as a guest bath. By hanging a bamboo shade or other screening device over the tub when the bath isn't needed, you can transform a bathroom into a powder room (see the bottom drawing on the facing page). Another strategy is to separate the shower or tub with a partition so that it's out of view.

If you eliminate unnecessary bathrooms, you'll save money and space. Use the space for a place just for yourself; and put the money toward making the bathrooms you do build more beautiful.

Sunroom or Porch?

What about those places in a house that serve no quantifiable function? The screen porch may seem to be just a place to enjoy a summer night. In a burst of practicality, many people decide during construction to make the porch all-season. It seems like

such a small change to add windows and doors, but the change will turn a place that would be used and cherished as a protected outdoor space into yet another sunny room in a house. A sunroom has a different function than a porch: A sunroom is an all-year-round indoor space, while a screen porch celebrates summer weather and the outdoors.

Newer houses in particular feature so many windows that several rooms in a typical house could be considered sunrooms already (see the photo below). In such a case, a sunroom often becomes yet another sitting room—beautifully appointed, but not much used. If your house has no similar space, a sunroom makes sense. One light-filled social space will get used, but two or more merely duplicate functions.

A screen porch isn't a luxury–it's an essential way to celebrate summer weather and the outdoors.

Living rooms in new houses often feature many windows. When you add a sunroom to such a house, it merely duplicates functions.

Older houses often have front porches that connect them to the street and the community beyond. In summer, the porch becomes the most cherished room in the house.

A porch doesn't have to be big. This three-sided porch, with elegant and minimalist detailing, transforms the house for summer living.

the thunderstorms and sunsets there. We were outside all the while, separated from nature by only a thin layer of mesh through which the mosquitoes could not penetrate. It very quickly became our favorite room in the house (see the photo on p. 57).

This experience is very different from sitting in a sunroom, which never gives you the impression you are actually outside, despite all the windows. The windows are a definite membrane between inside and outside. Even if you don't live in an area besieged with airborne pests, the experience of sitting on a

This writing nook offers a place for a poet to curl up on pillows and contemplate the view beyond.

In Minnesota, where I live, the summer season is short and the air is thick with mosquitoes. If we want to be outside during the summer, we must have a screened porch. When I first moved here, I didn't understand this and very nearly converted the porch on the front of the old house I had just purchased into an extension of the living room. Luckily, I didn't have enough money at the time to follow through with my plans. After just a few weeks of summer, I realized that the porch was the living area for the few months of good weather, between June and September. We ate there, socialized there, watched porch, outside but protected by a section of roof, is delightful. The more sides of the porch open to the great outdoors the better: one is hardly enough; two is better; three is ideal.

A Place of One's Own

Whenever you tinker in the garage or retreat to a sewing room, you're expressing the need for a place of your own. Children get their own rooms, but a couple tend to share all their space with each other. Joseph Campbell wrote this about the need for personal space: "You must have a room or a certain hour of the day or so where you do not know what is in the morning paper. A place where you can simply experience and bring forth what you are and what you might be. At first you may think nothing's happening. But if you have a sacred space and take advantage of it and use it everyday, something will happen" (quoted in *Simple Abundance*, Warner Books, 1995).

Perhaps the search for the essence of this place—a room of one's own—has contributed to the scale of houses today: More and more rooms are planned in an attempt to create distance and separation. But all that's necessary to create a place for yourself is a very small area—truly just big enough for one. Tucked into an attic or carved out of a bedroom, such a place should encourage you to be yourself. A writer and poet I know made her personal space in a corner of the master bedroom (see the bottom photo on the facing page). By extending the windows from floor level to 2 ft. 4 in. off the floor, she can sit on cushions on the floor and have a bird's-eye view of the outside world as she contemplates her next poem. My own private place is an attic hideaway, accessible by a ship's ladder.

The author's own private place is accessible with a ship's ladder. Carved into an attic, it's a place of quiet inspiration.

Both a place for meditation and for writing, it is filled with things that I love and that have special meaning to me. It is a true expression of my inner self: a place where I find inspiration, clarity, and focus.

"Do not keep anything in your home that you do not know to be useful or believe to be beautiful."—William Morris

Anyone who's ever spent time on a sailboat already appreciates how the Not So Big House works. Each space within the boat is carefully tailored to serve more than one function. Everything from recycling bins to clothes storage is well considered. Because of this careful, thoughtful use of space, it's no great exaggeration to suggest that six people can live more comfortably on a 40-ft. boat than they can in a big, badly designed house.

The same kind of thinking that makes a sailboat both habitable and sea-worthy can make a Not So Big House work. As you pare down the actual square footage of your house plan, think about how to make various areas do double duty. For example, in a boat, the seats to the dining table double as beds (see the top photo on p. 62). In a Not So Big House, the fireplace hearth can also become a seating area with the addition of cushions. While storage in a boat is carved out of every possible place, in the Not So Big House it's been carved into the

design of the house. When attention is paid to the usefulness of a house, there's a place for everything and everything is in its place. In architectural lingo, such a house expresses a "useful beauty."

But how do you make the Not So Big House work as efficiently as a 40-ft. boat? In this chapter, you'll learn about ways to make spaces do double duty, about planning for creative storage, and about strategies that will make your Not So Big House feel bigger. Through the alchemy of architecture, efficient smaller areas can be transformed into spacious, gracious spaces for living.

A wooden boat expresses the essence of Not So Big: a place for everything and everything in its place.

Like a boat, this living area provides places that can do double duty. The hearth, for example, can become extra seating with the addition of cushions.

This Japanese interior is a living room by day and a bedroom by night. The futons and bedding are kept hidden from view in cupboards.

Doing Double Duty

I once spent several weeks with a Japanese family as part of an academic exchange program. Their house was extremely compact—and the way the family made it work was to change the function of the rooms over the course of the day. By day, the room Westerners would call the living room was used for more formal sitting and adult conversation. At night, this room became the children's sleeping area. The bedding, which was stored behind sliding doors, came out at night, and was then rolled up again in the morning (see the photo above). My room, which was truly tiny by Western standards, served per-

fectly adequately as both my bedroom and my study, because I rolled up my bed as well.

Although I'm not advocating that our homes should be as compact as the average Japanese home, it does seem as if our rooms have grown bigger to accommodate various activities and all their related furnishings. Rather than make an area larger, think about ways spaces can be shared. A home office by day can serve as a bedroom by night. An informal dining area can easily be turned into a place for formal dining with the addition of dimmer-controlled lighting. Consider other ways of doubling up: Can the away room also be an office? Or is it a place to listen to music? Is the guest bedroom a good place to put the television? Can the laundry hallway double as a place for guests to put their suitcases?

Allowing areas in a house to "moonlight" is one way to make them do double duty. And in the Not So Big House, the spaces where most time is spent should be able to accommodate a range of activities. The way to do this is to create spaces within a larger area that can be transformed to serve different functions.

Shelter around Activity

Creating shelter around a specific activity is a concept children instinctively understand whenever they make cozy hideaways out of cardboard boxes. What they're doing is creating a smaller space within the larger confines of their rooms. Adults exhibit a similar need for shelter when they go to a restaurant. Imagine you've arrived for dinner and you're the only one in

Children like to make cozy spaces for themselves out of whatever material is handy—in this case, a cardboard box gives a sense of shelter.

the restaurant. The waitress seats you in the middle of the room, but, if you're anything like me, you'll most likely ask for a corner booth, which offers a sheltered place where you can enjoy the restaurant as it bustles into life.

The alcove is the adult's equivalent of the cardboard box. Walls wrap around three sides of the alcove just as a restaurant booth does. Alcoves are a fundamental strategy for making Not So Big work. And they can be placed in virtually any space, from living areas to bedrooms. A room that has an alcove automatically does double duty by providing an alternative space within a larger space. The living area shown in the photo at left has two alcoves. One contains a window seat and a rocking chair; the other is more adaptable, changing function to suit the occasion—in this instance, Lego play time.

The Third Dimension

A floorplan encourages us to think in only two dimensions—length and width. Placing walls and doors is the usual way spaces are defined within a house, so most people think that they've finished with the design process once the floorplan is set. But the height of these spaces is what makes places feel

An alcove will make any room do double duty by creating a space within a larger area. This room has two alcoves—one for reading and watching television, the other in use as play space.

comfortable or uncomfortable. Have you ever been in an office building with room after room of 8-ft. ceilings? Uniform ceiling heights make any space feel homogenous. By raising or lowering the ceiling, spaces are enlivened and places within the larger area are created that are individually defined yet clearly part of the whole. In the photo of the dining area at right the lowered ceiling functions as the brim around a hat does, marking space.

Many people feel more comfortable under a lowered ceiling. A friend who was remodeling a warehouse space contacted me for advice. The loft, which had great light, turned out to be virtually unusable. The space was long and narrow—almost like a bowling alley. The only places that my friend felt comfortable in were the corners, where the two walls offered some shelter. A simple, inexpensive solution was to lower the ceiling at both ends. What had been unusable space was transformed into three spaces that could house various activities. The height of a space is critical to how it is experienced: Make sure to include the third dimension of height in the planning process.

Ceiling Height

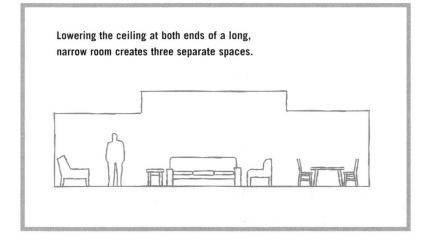

Lowering the ceiling at both ends of a long, narrow room creates three separate spaces.

The lowered soffit, put to use as a plate rail, gives a sense of shelter to the bench seating below.

Lighting for Formal Dining

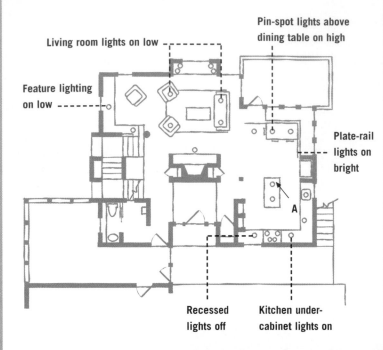

Living room lights on low

Feature lighting on low

Pin-spot lights above dining table on high

Plate-rail lights on bright

A

Recessed lights off

Kitchen under-cabinet lights on

Interior Lighting

Light is intrinsically connected to mood. A sunny day seems to express a cheerful mood, while a cloudy one might make us feel more introspective. Correspondingly, the use of light inside a house can transfigure a space. In the photos below, an everyday dining area is transformed by subdued lighting into an elegant place to entertain. By using brighter light, the same area can feed the family. Light is the primary tool for changing the mood of a space—and there are many sophisticated systems on the market that allow you to control each scene within the house with a series of dimmers (see the sidebar on p. 68).

Light can also be used to differentiate one place from another. If every area is lit to the same degree, a house can become very

Lighting is the most useful tool for creating interior ambience. Here, the lighting setting is for formal dining. The floorplan above shows how the various fixtures are set to create the appropriate mood. (Photo taken at A on floorplan.)

homogenous in mood and feeling. By lighting different areas with different intensities, various areas can be distinguished within a larger space.

Making More of the Practical

The year I turned 21, I spent part of the summer living with six other people on a 40-ft. sailboat. By day, we sailed the Puget Sound; each night, anchored by an island shore, we came to appreciate the level of detail in the boat's interior. Every square inch on the boat was lovely to look at—from the brass cleats on the bow to the vent stack in the latrine. As I design Not So Big Houses, I often think back to the level of detail on that boat and the ways it helped us live in relative harmony, despite

After-Dinner Lighting

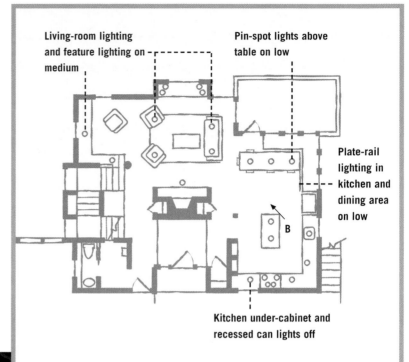

Living-room lighting and feature lighting on medium

Pin-spot lights above table on low

Plate-rail lighting in kitchen and dining area on low

B

Kitchen under-cabinet and recessed can lights off

After dinner, the lighting system allows for a quick change of scene. Now the living area is illuminated and the dining area is more subdued. (Photo taken at B on floorplan.)

Lighting-Control Systems

Newer houses are filled with lots of different kinds of lighting, such as wall sconces, recessed lights, and pin-spot lighting. But more often than not, the proliferation of switches simply makes it easier to turn everything on rather than try to remember which switch controls what light. I first realized the need for more central-ized control when designing light-ing systems for new homes. When I visited my clients after they'd spent some time living in their new houses I discovered that they simply turned everything on when they walked into a room, complete-ly negating the intended effect of having different lighting for differ-ent occasions.

There are a variety of lighting-control systems, which range in price, complexity, and flexibility. Some systems control the entire house, although these seem like overkill for the average home-owner. One house I recently designed for a couple included an expensive whole-house light-ing system. In the bedroom, three scenes were offered—evening reading, morning dressing, and cleaning. The system controlled only two fixtures,

however—recessed lights in the ceiling and bed-side lamps. The homeowners were confronted with a variety of choices every time they walked into their bedroom, none of which exactly fit their intentions. They spent time trying to rename the functions, when all that was really required was two simple switches on the wall. In their case, the lighting-control system was complicating their lives, not simplifying it.

The Lutron Grafik Eye System has six dimmer switches for different lighting loads.

I prefer systems that control the main living area of a house, allowing the homeowner to con-trol each "scene" by setting a series of dimmers that are then controlled by a single switch. Other systems allow even greater flexibility, but they require initial programming by a technician. These are signifi-cantly more expensive, and they offer more con-trol than most people find useful.

Within the next decade or so, some sort of lighting-control system will probably be installed in all new houses—in the main living areas, at the very least. Lighting-control systems are just the beginning of what will become standard for all new houses as we develop ways to monitor and control from a single centralized location.

its cramped quarters. A boat's function depends on the crafting of its details. A Not So Big House's graciousness and livability comes from careful consideration of everything from the back hallway to the finishing touches in the kitchen. The practical

places in a house, those unglamorous rooms where the work gets done, don't have to be unappealing. If you make the most of every space in a house—from the laundry room to the re-cycling center—you'll discover the joys of living Not So Big.

A laundry room
doesn't have to look
like a laundry room.
Here, a sewing room
also functions as a
folding area for an
adjacent washer/dryer.
(Photo taken at A on
floorplan.)

The Laundry Room

The laundry room is an itinerant space that travels upstairs and downstairs in floorplans, with no seemingly logical place to settle. In many older homes, it resides in the basement. In newer homes, it sometimes has its own spacious digs, complete with built-in folding and ironing equipment. The laundry room can also be found near the kitchen or adjacent to the master bedroom.

In designing a Not So Big House, I often ask clients a series of questions as we begin to think about the proper place for the laundry. Does it need to be an entire room, or could it be an alcove off a hallway? How much laundry does the household generate? Do you do large loads, or do you launder more frequently in smaller batches? Do you need an area to drip-dry

Laundry in the Sewing Room

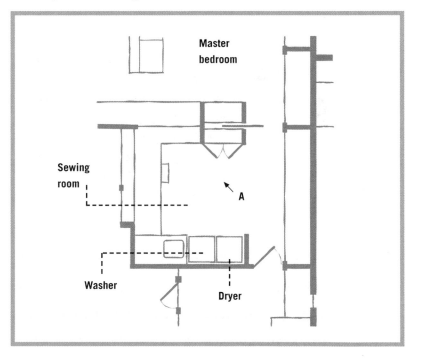

Laundry facilities can be no bigger than a closet. Here, a built-in counter serves as a place to fold laundry and also as a place for guests to put their suitcases. (Photo taken at A on floorplan.)

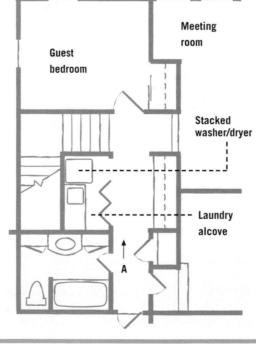

Hallway Laundry

Guest bedroom

Meeting room

Stacked washer/dryer

Laundry alcove

A

clothing? Would you prefer to fold clothes near the laundry area or elsewhere? Do you iron? If so, where do you like to iron?

Even though these questions prompt a variety of answers, one thing seems constant. While many people imagine they will do ironing and folding in the laundry area, they invariably take these activities elsewhere, either because they want to be near the rest of the family or because the laundry area is not a pleasant place to spend time in.

Depending on your lifestyle, there are various options for creating a place for the laundry. If you're an empty nester or a couple without children, a smaller area that's more similar to an alcove than a room (something adjacent to the master bedroom, perhaps) is adequate. Think about how the laundry area can be combined with another function: In the house shown on p. 69, it doubles as a sewing room. In my own house, the laundry alcove is covered with folding doors when it's not in use and simply blends into a hallway (see the photos on the facing page). A built-in counter along the hall can serve as a folding counter; and at other times it can offer a convenient place for guests to lay out their suitcases.

In some houses, the laundry doubles as the entrance from the garage. In this scenario, the main entrance takes everyone past piles of dirty clothes and detergent bottles. It's best to avoid placing the laundry here, but if it is the only spot you can find, it's a good idea to create a pleasant view to draw you beyond the clutter—either through a window or by hanging a favorite picture at the end of the way.

New Places for Not So New Things

What do junk mail, television, a bag of aluminum cans, a telephone, and a computer have in common? Each has no proper place in our homes. While the mail collects on the dining-room table and the cans accumulate in the kitchen, the computer resides in any number of places, from the office to the kitchen to the bedroom.

This mail center, located in a mudroom near the entrance, allows mail to be sorted and distributed to family members. The trash can is for recycling junk mail.

A Not So Big House includes space for each. A mail center near the entrance of the house (see the photo on p. 71) allows for separation of junk mail from bills and letters, which often end up in the kitchen. A kitchen mail center offers cubbyholes for each member of the family. And a kitchen island outfitted with trash cans can become a recycling center for cans and bottles.

A phone center can double as a kind of control panel for the house, hiding the thermostat and the air-quality and lighting-control system keypads (see the top left photo on the facing page). It can also house the calendar, family bulletin board, phone books, and address books. The use of a cordless phone keeps the area visually streamlined and allows for a minimum number of phone jacks in the house. The niche for the phone center shown in the photo was created from space in the fireplace chase. Its counterpart on the other end of the hearth is a broom closet. The wall on the backside of the fireplace defines the entry. The space between is filled with the main ductwork for the upper level of the house. In many houses, the bits and pieces of various controls are scattered throughout the building, for the convenience of the person who installs the system rather than for the long-term livability of the house. But this elegant solution brings all the controls together, mak-

A well-organized kitchen mail center has a cubbyhole for each family member. The work surface doubles as a place to pay bills.

Recycling for cans and bottles can take place where the waste is generated—here, it's in the kitchen island.

ing communication with the house and the rest of the world more efficient and more aesthetically pleasing.

As for the computer, it should find a place in the home that isn't makeshift. After all, the computer may be fairly new in our lives, but it is most definitely—in some form or fashion—here to stay. In designing a place for a computer, it's important to remember that printers, modems, external drives, manuals, disk files, and software boxes typically come with it—all of which need storage space in easy reach of the computer user. You can include space for the computer in a home office (see pp. 49-53), or you can put telephone jacks in public spaces where a laptop computer can hook into the Internet. As technology continues to introduce new tools into our lives, we must continue to update the way we think about the spaces we need in our houses.

In many houses, the real hearth of the home is the television. (Indeed, a recent best-selling video in Sweden was of a crackling fire!) The placement of the television often creates some acoustical and design challenges in the Not So Big House. The pattern of how the television is used is the best way to determine its placement. If watching television is an infrequent activity—or one that is more private—a good solution is to put it in a cabinet that can

This phone nook is the control center for the whole house, with phone, thermostats, and lighting and air-quality controls all consolidated.

The place for a computer doesn't need to be large, but you do need to plan for all the accompanying equipment.

In a room designed for television viewing as well as other activities, folding doors can conceal the set when it's not on.

In a room where television watching is the main event, the television and its surrounding cabinetry can be designed as a sculptural statement, as in this contemporary home.

be closed up, as shown in the photo at right on p. 73.

The family who owns the house shown in the photo on the facing page recognized that the television was the true hearth of their home. Rather than hide the television, they decided to make a sculptural statement with it. Its placement in the family area is actually adjacent to the fireplace, where family and friends can gather for either warmth or football, as the mood strikes. In my own house, I wanted to avoid having the blank face of the television staring at us at all times, tempting us to turn it on in our free moments. The wooden cabinet hides the television from the rest of the living area, while an alcove big enough for two allows us to keep the screen size small (see the top photo at right). Putting the television on a swivel base allows its position to be changed and lets it be seen from a variety of viewing points—a useful solution for media junkies (see the bottom photo at right).

When family members are trying to work or read, the noise of the television can be irritating. One solution is to create a space just for the television that can be closed off acoustically from the

Flanked by the side of a built-in cabinet, this television is designed to be visible only when sitting in an alcove. From the adjacent living area, you don't even know it's there.

A swivel base allows the television to be oriented toward different activity areas.

rest of the house (an away room). The key idea in creating a space for the television is to recognize your relationship to the TV—what it is and what you want it to be—and design accordingly.

Making Not So Big Feel Bigger

Square footage can be deceiving: Some big houses feel small, and some small houses feel big. The house shown in the top photo on p. 76 has a 900-sq.-ft. footprint, while the house shown in the photo below it has a 3,000-sq.-ft. footprint. The smaller space appears to be bigger because various strategies were employed to make it appear so. The image of the larger house feels smaller because views are kept short to create a sense of intimacy in the main living area. If you want to make Not So Big feel bigger, the following strategies will help you create a sense of spaciousness.

Diagonal Views

The diagonal line is used by both choreographers and theater directors to "activate the stage," in theater terminology. Similarly, architects use an imaginary diagonal line to create more dynamic

This small room feels big because there are long views sweeping from one corner of the house to the other.

This big room feels more cozy because the larger space is divided into smaller areas by the scale and place- ment of the fireplace.

A diagonal view, which stretches here from the kitchen to the piano alcove, not only makes a space seem bigger but also ensures that each area within is used on an everyday basis. The reason for this is simple: If you can see a space, you're more likely to use it.

spaces, which do in fact feel bigger. The reason for this is mathematical. Just as the hypotenuse of a triangle is the longest line, so in a square room, the diagonal view—from corner to opposite corner—is the longest dimension. If you create a number of diagonal views, you will focus on the longest view and so perceive the house to be larger than it is (see the photo above). Diagonal views can begin at the home's entrance. If you can

stand by the front door and see both opposite corners of the first floor, the house will automatically feel bigger. If you offer unobstructed sight lines to whatever space is diagonally opposite the kitchen, dining, and living areas, the house will seem bigger and more welcoming. When you see a space, you feel invited into it. And if you see a space, you use it more often.

Ceiling Height

A lowered soffit creates a pocket of coziness in a soaring space.

A ceiling trellis gives a sense of entry to the kitchen.

Why do we think that high ceilings make a space feel bigger than low ceilings? Our perception might come from hearing the basic measurement of the space: A room with an 18-ft.-high ceiling, for example, seems very big. And certainly, the volume of such a room will be bigger. But in some instances a high ceiling actually works against the perception of spaciousness.

In our architectural office, which is located in a renovated warehouse, the ceiling height in the conference room is 10 ft. 6 in. The footprint of the room is 10 ft. by 14 ft. When clients try to gauge the size of a space we've drawn for them, they often try to relate it to the dimensions of the conference room. But the ceiling height makes the room's floor area feel smaller than it would with an 8-ft. or 9-ft. ceiling. The reason for this is both mathematical and psychological. If the ceiling is the largest dimension, that is where our attention is drawn. We look up, marveling at ceiling height, instead of appreciating what the room has to offer at eye level. If the length and the width are longer than the height, then that is where our attention goes—the room feels longer and wider, hence bigger.

High ceilings are often considered more desirable than lower ceilings. This notion might come from a confusion between what is interesting and what is comfortable. Just because a chair is interesting to look at doesn't mean it's going to be comfortable to sit in. The same applies to a house. While we may reject a room with an 8-ft. ceiling because we perceive it to be run-of-the-mill, it can be more comfortable than a room with a high ceiling. Also, both high and low ceilings can be modulated with lowered areas. In the dramatic living room shown in the photo at left a lowered soffit creates a pocket of coziness within a soaring space. A ceiling trellis below a standard 8-ft.-high ceiling creates visual interest much less expensively than a 9-ft. or 10-ft. ceiling would.

Remember, though, that the proportion of the ceiling height to other dimensions of the room is important. A 10-ft. ceiling might feel right in a 25-ft.-wide room, but it can turn a powder room into an elevator shaft. Similarly, an 8-ft. ceiling in a large room will make the space feel like a generic office building.

And, obviously, if you're tall, an area with a 7-ft. ceiling may not feel comfortable. Frank Lloyd Wright, a man who stood 5 ft. 5 in. high, used lower ceilings throughout his houses and other buildings, believing if it worked for him it should work for everyone. In fact, his taller patrons find his architecture to be constricting.

Generous circulation spaces are critical to building Not So Big: A few extra feet at the top of the stairs can make all the difference. With a barrel-vaulted ceiling, this stair landing is a defined place, instead of just a passageway to somewhere else.

Generous Circulation

In planning a Not So Big House, don't sacrifice square feet at the entry and in passageways. When you enter a house that doesn't give you enough room to comfortably take off your coat or move about, you automatically feel confined and unwelcome. While realistically there doesn't need to be a large amount of space at the front of the house, the proportion of the entrance can set the tone for the rest of the house. A large house with too-small circulation spaces makes you feel as if you're in a small house. Similarly, a smaller house with generous circulation areas feels bigger.

A few well-placed square feet can turn a stairwell into a stairway. The upstairs landing should beckon you with light; it should feel like a place in which there is generous room to move. Narrow hallways use up square footage that is better applied to living spaces. If you must have a hallway, find ways to introduce light into it, or put a lighted picture at the end so that you have something to walk toward.

Natural light in hallways makes them seem both wider and more inviting. Imagine this same space without the windows, and it would become almost tunnel-like.

Windows frame the view outside and can also make a striking interior composition. Glass block used as a border creates a geometric pattern.

Let There Be Daylight

Light is integrally connected to our perception of space. Of all the qualities that people desire in a house, "light-filled" is among the most popular. Daylight, in obvious ways, makes a house feel welcoming. Windows connect us to the world, and by carefully planning their placement we can fill our houses with light and views. In Colonial times, fresh air was consid-

ered dangerous—and virtually windowless houses were shut tight at night to keep out the evil wind. Two hundred years ago, glass was expensive and difficult to find, and windows were used in construction quite sparingly. In the past 70 years, the number of windows used in construction has increased dramatically. But just like square footage, the number of windows does not necessarily make a house feel big. That's a function of how the windows are placed.

When placing a window, think of it not only as a frame for an exterior view but also as an interior composition, a kind of painting that is part of the wall. In the photo shown at left, a square window surrounded by glass block allows both views and a pattern of light to stream in. The window also functions as an important part of the living area's composition.

If you want good views of the outside, windows are best placed no more than 2 ft. 6 in. off the floor. If windows are higher than that, the view of the outside is limited—when seated you won't be able to see anything below the horizon line. This creates a sense of disconnection with the ground on which the house sits, a disconcerting effect similar to when you were a child sitting at the table, legs dangling, straining to reach the plate and see out of the window. In bedrooms, lower levels, and all seating areas, windowsills should be brought down so they don't obstruct views; by adjusting the sill, a connection to the outdoors is ensured.

Corner windows, two windows that come together in a corner, extend the diagonal views to the horizon. While a window in a flat surface defines only one direction, a corner window presents no boundaries to the view. A window that's placed right up to the edge of a ceiling without a frame makes a space

Windows placed up against the ceiling without frames make a space feel bigger because light bounces off the ceiling and walls.

feel bigger, because it becomes part of both the wall and the ceiling. In the photo on p. 81, the light reflected on the ceiling is a direct result of the window placement. Without the typical shadow cast by a window frame, the effect is striking: The ceiling seems to float. The window is simply a membrane between inside and outside, merely a surface that is a part of the wall. In fact, if you think about windows as see-through walls, then you can extend the connection between inside and outside (as shown in the photo below).

Sliding Doors

For many years pocket doors were flimsy contraptions outfitted with cheap hardware, which meant that the doors constantly fell off their tracks. The sliding door has come a long way: With heavy-duty hardware, any door can now be converted into a fail-safe sliding door.

The main reason to use a sliding door is to save space. There are areas of the house where the addition of the space needed for a swinging door would feel awkward. A 3-ft.-wide powder

The frameless windows in this house dissolve the separation between inside and out.

Sliding doors save space and are particularly useful in a small powder room. (Photo taken at A on floorplan.)

Powder Room with Sliding Door

Interior Views

Houses are usually designed to take advantage of outside views, with windows in just the right places to capture various scenes within the landscape. But we also spend a great deal of time looking within the house, and the composition of "interior views" is equally important. While a window frames an exterior view, ceilings and the edges of walls and floors frame interior views. If these views are thoughtfully composed, the house becomes beautiful to look at, from the armchair by the hearth or, as shown here, from the front entry through the living room.

The focal point of this interior view is a fireplace, framed by beams, columns, and the stair landing.

room, for example, won't accommodate the swing of a hanging door (see the photo and plan on p. 83). Sliding doors work particularly well in narrow spaces and in hallways (to hide laundry facilities, for example). In fact, the sliding door is an easy way to hide many different spaces you want kept out of view. A mudroom could have a sliding door, as could the kitchen, to conceal it when guests are over for dinner.

Connecting to the Outdoors

A Not So Big House will feel bigger if spaces for living are created outside as well as inside. As we saw in Chapter 2, porches and decks can increase living space considerably, especially in areas where weather isn't a great concern. When the roof offers shelter over the deck, the area becomes integrated with the rest of the house. And the extension of the roof line actually makes the house seem bigger from the inside. The courtyard house

The inspiration for this Minnesota house was an Italian cloister. With broad overhangs and precast concrete columns, a covered walkway connects the house with the outdoors.

shown in the photos on these two pages was designed for a Minnesota woman who loves Italian architecture. Taking as inspiration the Italian cloister, the plan of the house allows for two circulation patterns—one inside, with views of the courtyard, and one outside, with views of the passageway. Two sides of the house are open and two sides are interior, allowing

the house to project its Italian image while making it useful in a northern climate. The seating area beneath the roof gives the sense of being inside, protected from the elements, but with views to the garden courtyard. From the inside, looking out, there is a layering of places that range from completely interior to partly exterior to completely exterior.

Creative Storage

While storage in many homes takes the form of a closet, in a Not So Big House storage is a strategic defense against clutter. In a Not So Big House, storage is designed for the way you live and the things you do. The hierarchy of how often the things in your life are used—from every day, to once in a while, to never—influences how storage is planned in a Not So Big House. William Morris, one of the founders of the Arts and Crafts movement, proclaimed 100 years ago: "Do not keep anything in your house that you do not know to be useful or believe to be beautiful." Such is the organizing principle behind storage in the Not So Big House: Every space is considered for what is useful; special places are planned to display what is beautiful.

The outside cloister is echoed inside by a long passageway filled with arched windows. It's the cold-weather alternative to the outside walkway.

85

In each instance, storage corresponds to the place where the object is used: from a drawer in a window seat to a broom closet set into the fireplace area. Remember that the budget for your house will make an impact on the kind of storage you choose. Built-ins, in general, add significant cost to the overall price of the house. Very generally, you can assume that the cost will be analogous to a purchased piece of furniture of similar quality.

Creative Kitchens

In a Not So Big House, the kitchen is open to the living areas, so storage is essential to the way the kitchen functions and looks. The pantry is a very useful space: Make it as big or as small as necessary to fit the way the kitchen is used. If you are a gourmet cook, the pantry will be scaled to accommodate specialty items and equipment. If you'll use the pantry every day,

Pantries don't have to be walk-in size to be useful. A very efficient way to store kitchen supplies is to line a hallway with a pantry wall. In this instance, a 15-in.-wide dividing wall is a pantry on one side and bookshelves on the other. (Photo taken at A on floorplan.)

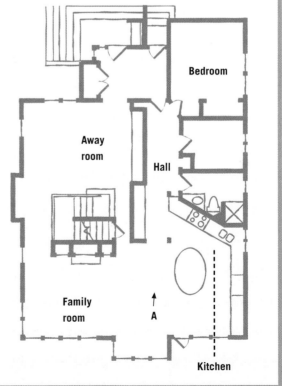

make it part of the kitchen. If you hoard items—buying jars of jam for next Christmas—it can be its own walk-in area.

The hallway that separates the kitchen area from the away room in the photo above is designed as a highly creative storage area (another example of "doing double duty"). The dividing wall, which is only 15 in. wide, becomes a very useful pantry area for the kitchen and creates bookshelf space for the

An L-shaped corner pantry was created from a former powder room in this kitchen remodeling. No bigger than a closet, it enhances the storage capacity of the kitchen.

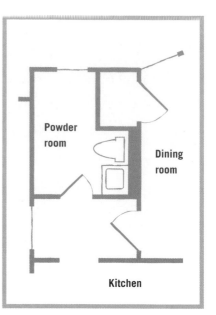

Powder room

Dining room

Kitchen

Creating Pantry Space: Before

away room. Walls at the edge of a circulation space can easily become fabulous pantries with the addition of 10 in. in depth (the width of a typical cereal box). In many ways, this is the most efficient kind of kitchen storage. Shallow storage makes everything visible and reachable.

The pantry shown in the photos and drawings on these two pages was literally carved out of a corner. It's no bigger than

3 ft. by 3 ft. and uses space that was formerly part of the powder room. Despite its odd shape, the pantry greatly enhances the storage capacity of the kitchen.

Another defense against kitchen clutter is the appliance garage (see the photo on p. 90). In recent years, the number of available kitchen implements has reached epic proportions. An appliance garage can hide appliances such as toasters,

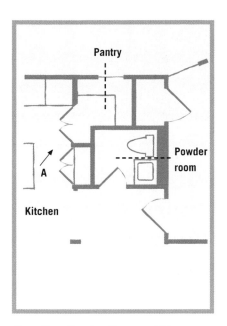

Creating Pantry Space: After

Although the pantry is oddly shaped, when the doors are closed it integrates perfectly with the rest of the kitchen. (Photo taken at A on floorplan.)

juicers, and breadmakers from view, yet keep them within easy reach.

The philosophy of the Not So Big House advocates that the things you use everyday are those things that have the most meaning. A client, planning for her retirement house, wanted a built-in cabinet in the dining room to store her heirloom china, which she planned on giving to her children. But while the fancy china had been cherished, it had never been used, so her adult children had no childhood memories of it. We decided to store most of the china in the basement, and made a special hutch in the kitchen to display a few choice pieces.

Most people would relegate the space under the stairs to a coat closet. But English designer John Ferro Sims transformed the space under the stairs in the London studio of the noted

Strategies for avoiding kitchen clutter include a hanging pot rack, a center island, and an appliance garage in the corner. Stacking the microwave and wine storage above the appliance garage makes optimum use of a corner space.

90

The space under the stairs in a London studio has been turned into a small jewel of a kitchen.

sculptor Henry Moore into a tiny but elegantly efficient kitchen (see the photo above and on p. 60). What most of us would consider wasted space becomes innovation at its finest in the hands of this designer. Here we see the very essence and personality of the Not So Big House.

Innovative Everyday Closets and Cupboards

Consider the convenience of having the extra roll of toilet paper where it's needed, instead of down the hallway. Storage in the living areas of the Not So Big House is always a convenient and sometimes obvious solution to an everyday problem

that can leave us stranded—pants around ankles—waddling to the laundry room.

The bedroom storage in the photo below shows the foresight of careful planning. In a bedroom that has limited space, the closet was designed to use every cubic inch to maximum effect. Built-ins, shelves, and mirrors, all behind folding doors, store clothes and personal items. This room does double duty: When the closet doors are closed and the futon is folded into a couch,

Consider putting storage where it's useful—adjacent to the toilet, for example.

This room is a symphony of storage. With built-in dressers, shelves, and mirrors, all enclosed in a wall cabinet, the room can do double duty as a bedroom or an away room. Notice the light fixture above the mirror—an ingenious way to give light where it's needed.

it functions as an away room. But with futon down and closet doors open, it becomes a combined bedroom and dressing area. The closet addresses a problem common with mirror placement. The recessed lights and the mirror are actually attached to the back of the door, ensuring that the light is in the proper location for using the mirror. In the bedroom shown below, built-in storage surrounds a fireplace hearth. Functional and beautiful, it becomes an integrated piece of the room's design.

Above: Windows, mirror, medicine cabinet, and sink are each typically given their own wall space. Here, they all happily coexist in an innovative design.

Left: Built-in storage around a fireplace makes a beautiful statement in a bedroom.

Any corner, nook, or cranny can function as storage.
Here, the kneewall has become a triangular storage area;
drawers under the window seat store blankets.

A common problem in bathroom design is the conflict between medicine cabinet, window, and mirror. Typically in new homes, the mirror takes up most of the wall surface above the sink, allowing little space for a medicine cabinet or window. People often assume that they can't put a window into the wall behind a sink because they need it for the mirror. But, in fact, the mirror doesn't need to be wall-sized. By breaking every rule in the book, the solution shown in the photo at right on p. 93 accommodates all three functions on one wall surface.

The guest coat closet is often scaled to accommodate 25 coats. The reality is that it is usually empty, or crammed with last year's Christmas wrapping paper and newspapers awaiting recycling. When guests do arrive, they typically traipse upstairs to pile coats on a bed. When you plan for coat closets in a Not So Big House, put them next to the front door. The closet doesn't need to be enormous, just big enough. When large groups of people visit, all the coats go into a bedroom.

Remember that the guest closet in the Not So Big House is only for guests: Your coats go into the mudroom.

You can't predict what you'll need to store in the next five years. But when you design your Not So Big House, keep in mind that storage needs increase the longer you live in a house. In the left photo above, the kneewall area could have simply been walled over. By putting doors to access the area, it becomes unusually shaped, but still useful storage.

Double-Duty Storage

Any space in a Not So Big House is fair game for storage, especially in living areas. The strategy is to find a spot that seems to take up no extra square footage. The bunk bed shown in the photo above doubles as a blanket or toy chest. Drawers in window seats and benches are a more practical solution than a lift-up lid, which is troublesome to raise when cushions are set on top of it. Stairways can offer wall space that is easily trans-

Above: The stairway doesn't have to be just an unadorned passageway. In this house, it's become a library. While the shelves offer storage, the books become a kind of decoration, visible from upstairs and down.

Left: This bed could easily be on a boat. Carved into a corner, it's surrounded by drawers and shelves, offering a maximum of storage in a minimum of space.

In the Not So Big House, even the space under the stairs can provide storage—in this instance, for shoes.

Storage can also serve as display. A plate rail that lines the kitchen shows off a collection of handcrafted plates. The rail continues into the dining area, artfully linking the two rooms.

formed into bookshelves with the addition of 10 in. to the width of the stairwell. The area under the stair steps is frequently unused, particularly in houses without basements. As shown in the photo on the facing page, one enterprising designer used the space effectively for pull-out shoe storage.

Storage as Display

A useful addition to a dining area or kitchen is a plate rail, which offers both storage and display. The plates that line the rail in the kitchen area shown in the photo above are both beautiful and useful. With dramatic lighting, they become a work of art, but on many occasions the plates are taken from the rail to adorn the table as functional items.

A client who had an amazing collection of beer cans asked for a built-in display in a recreation area (see the photo at right). A music-loving client wanted storage for his collection

Any collection is fair game for display. Here's a wainscot of beer cans.

When planning for storage, think beyond the confines of the cupboard. Beautiful things should be seen and displayed for everyday enjoyment.

Storage for a collection of CDs becomes a kind of wallpaper lining the room.

of CDs. By lining the walls, they become a kind of wallpaper for the room where he likes to sit and listen to music (see the photo at right above). If you have a collection of items, whatever they may be, that collection expresses something about who you are. It's an opportunity to integrate into the house the things that inspire you and give you pleasure. A Not So Big House gains its personality from the passions of its inhabitants.

In the built-in pantry by designer Fu Tung Cheng shown on the facing page, concrete, Douglas fir, and steel are combined to create a work of usable sculpture. That something as commonplace as a pantry can be transformed into such a beautiful object expresses the potential of how storage in our houses can enhance the experience of living in them.

In this built-in pantry, natural materials and elegant design create usable sculpture.

> *"Home is an invention on which*
> *no one has yet improved."*
>
> —Ann Douglas

Early in my career I worked with a young couple who were both successful professionals in the computer-software business. They saw in their future a big new house where they would live for the rest of their lives. They planned to have two children, at some indefinite point in their lives, so they would need two extra bedrooms—plus a guest bedroom—in addition to their own. The couple were convinced that their yet-to-be-born children would have no effect on their current lifestyle. In fact, to maintain their own privacy, they wanted to put the kids' bedrooms at the opposite end of the house from the master bedroom.

Anyone who has ever lived with small children will immediately understand that this approach to bedroom location is completely unrealistic. The direct result of placing a young child's bedroom far from the parents' is that the child will move into the parents' bedroom—for months, sometimes even for years. But my clients were undeterred; their vision of an existence unfettered by children

This house, at 800 sq. ft., is truly Not So Big. Designed for one person, it embraces the solitude of living in the woods. With its north face tucked into the hill, the house offers an enigmatic first glance as you approach.

remained. We began to design a house that had the bedrooms where they wanted them. Rather sneakily, I added a sitting room off the master bedroom, which was separated from the bedroom by French doors. I knew that this would, most likely, become the nursery. And I decided to let them discover this for themselves.

The one thing that's predictable about life is that it's unpredictable. You can have a little control, however. The process of making a house Not So Big allows you to tailor the house to your needs and to create spaces that can easily adapt and change with you throughout the stages of your life. In this

chapter, we'll look at a number of houses, each designed for people with distinctly different lifestyles: From a retreat for a single professional to a remodeling for empty nesters, these Not So Big Houses express the values and passions of their inhabitants. Although none of the homeowners are exceptionally wealthy, they've all built houses that work for them and that have enriched their lives.

A House for One

The little house that Kelly Davis designed for himself expresses his love of solitude and small scale. Davis, who is a partner in our architectural firm, is convinced that small spaces are more conducive to such everyday activities as reading, conversation, and quiet evenings in front of the fire, so he decided to design a house that was no bigger than 800 sq. ft. Fascinated with how space can be made to appear larger than it is, he was determined to create a warm, intimate house that would be as fluid and unconfining as possible.

The site Davis found to build on, just a few miles from his office, was a 35-acre mix of woods and fields on the Wisconsin side of the St. Croix River that overlooks the river valley and a distant limestone bluff. Capturing this view was essential, but he also wanted to make certain that the house would be protected on blustery winter nights. The house is, in effect, notched into the hillside: sheltered from the north winds by a windowless wall and a low shed roof, while the south side opens up with large windows and a clerestory to let in views, light, and warmth.

Davis has traveled widely and admires the traditional architecture of Japan. He used as inspiration for his house the

Japanese concept of revealing vistas gradually, culminating in an element of surprise. The first indication of this is where cars park—at a garage/studio/guest room that's set about 300 ft. from the house. The only approach to the house is on foot, a kind of meditative walk through the woods that offers glimpses of the house and the view beyond (see the photo on the facing page). The house itself is a dramatic statement, with its powerful massing and sculptural form. Davis sustained this drama by setting the front door in a 7-ft.-wide alcove in the southeast corner of the house. (It's interesting to note that Kelly realized

that if he had placed the garage next to the house, it would have dwarfed the 800-sq.-ft. footprint.)

Inside, the house's open plan presents a feeling of spaciousness (see the photo and floorplan on p. 104). Long views extend from every direction, and a 50-ft.-long, 8-ft.-wide deck that's cantilevered over the hillside visible from the living area frames a view that's almost 75 ft. long from the living-room wall to the end of the deck. The living area of the house is anchored by a massive concrete fireplace, and spaces within it are defined by alcoves and built-in furniture, all of which is scaled appropriately to the house.

A soaring ceiling in the living area descends to create a sense of shelter for the built-in couch.

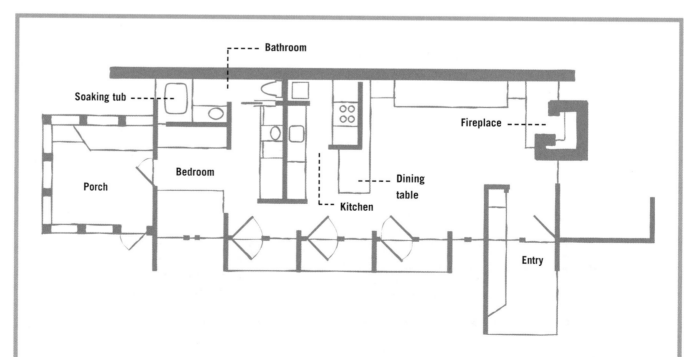

Bathroom

Soaking tub

Fireplace

Porch

Bedroom

Dining table

Kitchen

Entry

The small kitchen is screened from view by a partial wall but remains connected with the dining and living areas. The table can function as a countertop extension for the kitchen or as an eating area.

The bedroom, which is down a short, flat-ceilinged passageway, is hidden from the living area by a wing wall (see the photo on p. 106). A beautifully crafted bathroom connects to the bedroom. Davis wanted his house to be a retreat from the workaday world, so he purposefully did not include space for a drafting table and, hence, work he might otherwise have brought home. But a built-in desk and shelves in the bedroom allow the room to do double duty as an office where he manages his bills and correspondence. Should the need arise, the house is designed to accommodate the addition of a second bedroom and bath to the north of the existing bathroom. With an incredibly efficient use of space, and an impeccable eye for detail, this house is the epitome of Not So Big.

Because this is a house for one, there was no need to create acoustical privacy. The dining area is marked by a built-in table that's connected to the kitchen, which itself is partially shielded from the living area by a half-wall. Throughout the house, varied ceiling heights create shelter around specific activities and help activate the spaces: A soaring ceiling in the center of the living area is in contrast to a low ceiling along the north wall, which gives a more intimate feel to the sitting area. Wherever possible, Davis extended the inside to the outside. Windows are installed without frames, and a porch off the bedroom (shown in the photo at right) offers striking views in the summer months, as well as becoming a warm-weather bedroom. The roof, which cantilevers off the front and back of the house, also extends the impression of the house's size.

A screen porch located off the bedroom is for warm-weather sleeping; it's also a good place to enjoy striking views of a river valley.

The bedroom is really just an alcove, with a built-in bed sheltered by a lowered ceiling. The screen porch is beyond.

Designing for yourself can be both exhilarating and scary. While you can literally do anything that your budget allows, there's no one to discuss the ideas with; no one to counter your wishes. The challenge in this process is to realize that even if you now intend to live alone in the house for the rest of your life, the house can be a burden to sell if you make it too unique to your needs. Several years ago, I designed a house for a single man who wanted only one bedroom because he never had visitors. He had enough disposable income so that resale value wasn't a concern. He went ahead and planned for a single bedroom, complete with a whirlpool tub actually in the room. He saw no need for doors and, thus, the master bedroom (and its tub) was open to the living area below. A year after the house was finished, he fell in love. Unfortunately, his new partner did not have the same affection for his new house. The house went on the market, and stayed there for quite some time until an appropriate buyer came along, who was willing to remove the tub and add some doors, walls, and a guest bedroom.

When you're single, there's always the chance that the same thing could happen to you. When designing a home for one, how do you take into account the possibility for a change in relationship status? My suggestion (just as with designing for retirement years) is not to try to second-guess the future. Design sensibly, allowing the house to work for one or for two, but don't go overboard. My experience as an architect suggests that most new partners, when they move into a house that is so clearly an expression of the other's personality, will want a different space that expresses both personalities—even if the existing house is beautiful and comfortable.

This bathroom, complete with soaking tub, an abundance of natural woodwork, and a visible connection to the outdoors, reflects the owner's love for Japanese aesthetics.

Another thing to remember when designing for one is to make places that feel good to be alone in. To do this, select the two or three activities you enjoy doing most in the house and design places for those activities. Make sure there's a sense of shelter around each one. Even if you sit in a smaller space watching television or reading, you look out into the larger, more open spaces in the house. There's a big difference between being alone and feeling lonely—and nothing accentuates loneliness more than broad, open expanses of space. Smaller, more cozy places evoke a sense of security and introspection.

A House for a Couple with No Kids

If a couple isn't planning to have children and is designing a house for themselves, the stereotypical plan of "three bedrooms up" really doesn't make sense. Obviously, a house for two does not need to be as big as a house for a family with children and, in fact, can be much more comfortable if spaces are scaled appropriately. While an away room is usually unnecessary, work spaces are usually important to the plan. Though some couples can easily share an office, often each will take a differ-

This contemporary Prairie-style house on a river bluff was originally designed as a second home for a professional couple. It's now a full-time residence.

ent approach to organization. Recognizing these differences can help avoid a lot of potential arguments. Offices can also be useful for resale, especially when they can be easily converted into bedrooms. If you want an office to be able to function as a bedroom, make sure a closet is included or can easily be added later. When a couple are the sole inhabitants of a house, it is important to make sure that some spaces are comfortable for one or two people only.

The house shown at left was built by a professional couple in their mid-50s (Dianne and Bob) who approached me after months spent trying to design their second home themselves. They owned property on a river bluff, and they wanted a contemporary home that would be very different from the traditional house they owned in the city. However, both had strong opinions—strong and conflicting opinions. They needed an architect who could help give shape to their dreams and find common ground for both of them. The photos they had collected and brought to our planning sessions reflected their desire for everything to be open and visible. So the first design for their weekend house had a totally open floorplan with a wall of windows across the front of the house. While this seemed to be exactly what they wanted, I was concerned about

The relatively simple cubic form of this house allowed the owners to put more of their budget into windows. The living area features a wall of windows that captures a panoramic view. A window seat helps modulate the open expanse of space.

the lack of definition between the kitchen, eating, and living areas. An easy solution that maintains the sense of openness was to add a window-seat alcove in the middle of the wall of windows, directly across from the front door (see the photo on p. 109). The window seat beckons from the entry and also frames the spectacular outdoor views. Two built-in cabinets, designed especially for Dianne's collection of ceramic objects, flank the entrance to the living room, creating a kind of gateway into the main living spaces (see the photo on p. 100).

The form of the house is very simple, essentially a cube with two bays—one off the kitchen and the other in the window seat. Both bays extend the three stories of the house, providing alcoves in the kitchen, master bedroom, living room, and family room. The reason for the simple form of the house was economic: They wanted to devote as much of their budget as possible to windows in order to make the most of their spectacular view.

Specifically, the house was designed to take advantage of sunsets. Even the couple's bed is oriented toward the windows. But although there's a lot of glass, bands of trim and mullions help modulate the expanse of view, which creates smaller segments to frame the panorama. Without the trim and mullions,

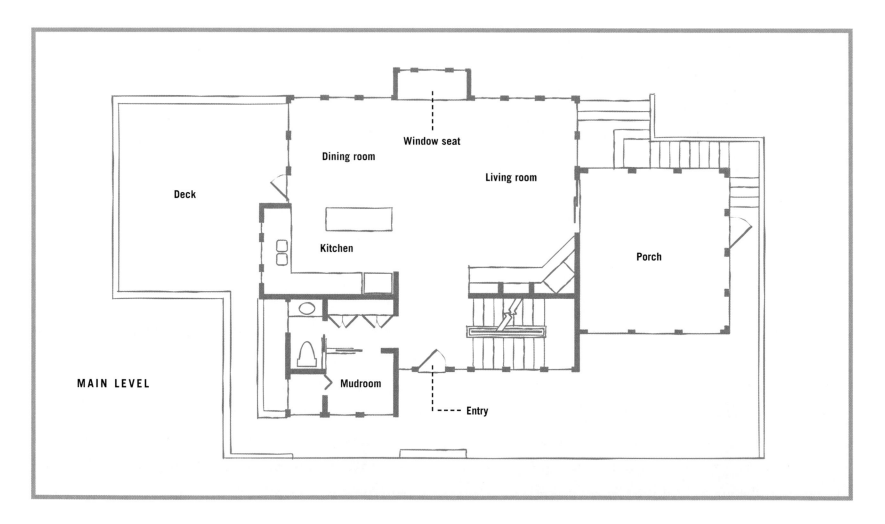

The kitchen's design is simple, with a minimum of detail. The main feature is a large window bay, which looks into the woods.

a large expanse of glass might make the homeowners feel as though they were living in a glass house.

The house—designed as it was to take advantage of the site—also had to function as a place where two professionals could take work home and actually get work done. Dianne wanted her office to be part of the rest of the house, and so we attached it to the master bedroom (see the photo on p. 112).

In many houses designed for couples without children, the main area of the house becomes what *A Pattern Language* refers to as "The Couple's Realm." The entire upstairs becomes the couple's suite, which is also a good place to put an office as well as a beautiful bathroom and generous walk-in closets. Dianne's work alcove offers her privacy and the best views in the house. Bob's office is a more defined room, located off the other side

An alcove in the master bedroom serves as an office area. The alcove is created by a lowered ceiling and a window bay that extends to two stories—on the first floor it accommodates a kitchen bay (see the photo on p. 111).

of the bedroom and attached to the bedroom with a sliding door. For Bob, the room becomes a kind of away room, offering acoustical privacy when he listens to music. Originally, the view wasn't as important to him as it was to Dianne. But, in fact, the view from Bob's study is quite lovely, and over time he's claimed the room as a place of his own.

The lower level is a basement on the bluff side of the house but completely exposed on the river elevation. Dianne and Bob often entertain out-of-town visitors, so both wanted to provide guests with their own spacious digs, allowing for privacy on both levels. With a family area, guest room, and bunk beds for kids, the lower level can easily accommodate an entire visiting family. Bunk beds, which take up only 18 sq. ft.,

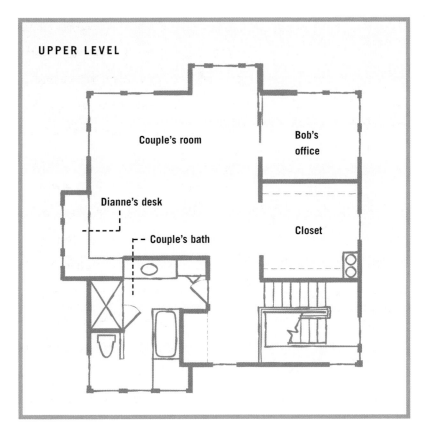

UPPER LEVEL

Couple's room

Bob's office

Dianne's desk

Couple's bath

Closet

has views of the river valley—it feels like a weekend home, but it's convenient for more than weekend life. Although my husband and I were initially concerned about the extra cost of a city lot, when we factored in the expense of having both a city residence and a country residence, the city lot seemed like the more cost-effective solution.

When people begin planning a second home they often automatically think in more informal terms, allowing themselves to envision options that they might not even consider for their primary residence. The architects in our firm have designed many second homes. Again and again my colleagues and I discover that our clients are much more comfortable in their second homes than they are in their primary ones. For that reason, the second, or weekend, home is one of the biggest inspirations

take the place of an additional bedroom (see the floorplan at right).

The house has changed Bob and Dianne's lives. After a year spent in their Not So Big House, designed to express their personalities and accommodate their needs, they decided to make this second home their primary residence. They still commute to the city for work, but they've completely downscaled and now stay in a small apartment while they wait for the weekend. Their retreat has become their home; and this is where their hearts are.

While Bob and Dianne found their dream site outside of a city, many people who are interested in building a weekend home have discovered the appeal of building a retreat inside the city. My own Not So Big House is located on a city site that

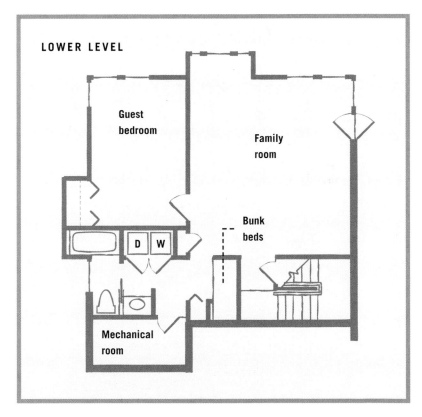

LOWER LEVEL

Guest bedroom

Family room

D   W

Bunk beds

Mechanical room

for the Not So Big House. The appeal of these weekend homes often is not just the location but the structure itself, which is designed to be comfortable, useful, and informal.

A House for a Family

Michaela Mahady, a partner in our firm, likes to encourage her clients and her students to capture the memory of houses from their past. Teaching a class on housing at the University of Minnesota, she encouraged her students to remember a place that had been important and to try and capture its essence. One of her students, Caroline, brought to class an intricate and beautiful collage of the house she had grown up in France. Ten

years later, Caroline and her husband, Peter, asked Mahady to help them design a house that would both express the charm of her childhood home and embrace the life of their young family.

Mahady, along with architect Wayne Branum, discovered that Caroline, a poet, and Peter, who is in the food commodities business, were able to articulate clearly the qualities they wanted in their new home. These included a home that felt like a tree house, a house where the family could dance together, and a house where daily life would happen in one spacious room. The site, quite wooded, also provided views of a small pond, and the architects knew that the family would want to be connected with the outdoors wherever possible.

The family who built this house not only wanted a beautiful place for daily life but also a room where they could dance together. The slate swath through the dining-area floor doubles as a dance floor, while the open living area is the core of the house.

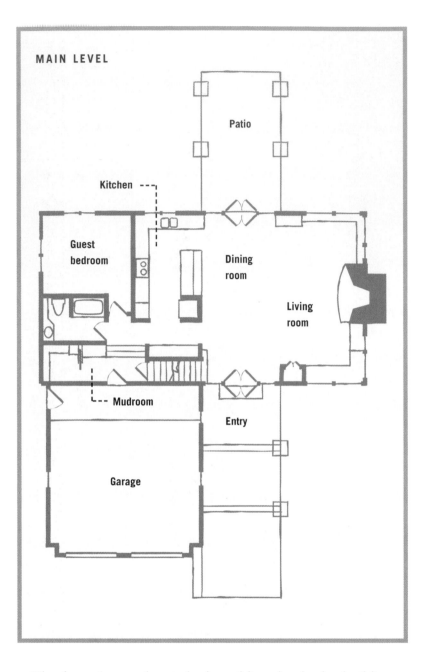

MAIN LEVEL

Patio

Kitchen

Guest bedroom

Dining room

Living room

Mudroom

Entry

Garage

The kitchen completes the center for daily life. Open to the living area, its design enhances the first floor. The owners have personalized it with various collections, from dried flowers to cheese boxes.

The house's steeply pitched roof line lends the building a European flair, but inside the house materials such as Brazilian cherry and China green slate give a more contemporary flavor. The one room for daily living that Caroline and Peter requested offers a perfect example of designing Not So Big. The kitchen is open to the dining and living areas. Variations in flooring material and ceiling height, as well as alcoves, help define places within the large space. A green slate floor marks the dining area, which is also the "dance floor" the clients requested (see the photo on p. 115). The slate, which offers a stunning contrast to the Brazilian cherry on the living and kitchen floors, continues outside, as do the wooden beams, extending the space visually at both the front and back of the house and making an area where the family can dance outside. A cathedral ceiling over the fireplace creates a dramatic vault that is in contrast to lowered ceilings in the kitchen and dining area, as well as over the corner window seats. The architects integrated the kitchen visually by using the distinctive green slate of the floor as a backsplash and natural wood cabinets that echo the wooden beams (see the photo above).

With its steep pitched roof, the house has a European flair. One of the owners wanted to capture the essence of a childhood home in France. The slate floor continues outside, offering patio space in the warmer months.

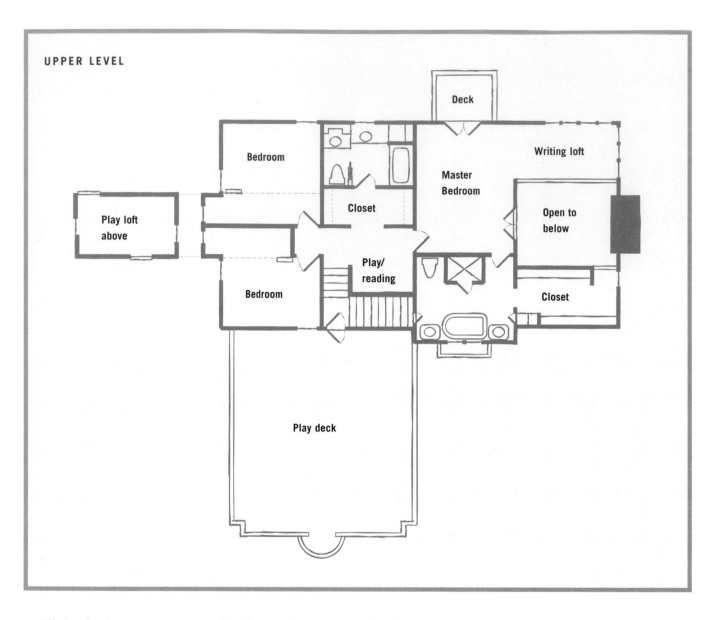

Deck

Bedroom

Writing loft

Master
Bedroom

Closet

Play loft
above

Open to
below

Play/
reading

Bedroom

Closet

Play deck

While the house encourages family togetherness on the first floor, upstairs it offers more private spaces, as well as places for both adults and children to play. Caroline and Peter's space contains a bedroom, a place of one's own for Caroline, who loves to sit on the floor and write, and a shared master closet and bathroom. Separated from the children's area by a door, the couple's realm is perched over the first-level living space, offering connection and privacy. A shared loft playroom con-

nects the two children's bedrooms (see the photo at left on the facing page) and is accessible by a ship's ladder. The stair landing has become another play space, at least in the winter, supplanted in warmer months by an outdoor area on the top of the garage: Shaded with colorful awnings in the summertime, it is a playground nestled into the treetops.

Since it was built in 1995, the house has become an even more personal expression of the family who lives there. With

Upstairs, there are places for children and adults to play. A shared loft playroom, accessible by a ship's ladder from the elder child's bedroom, connects the two children's bedrooms.

planned certain spaces for certain activities, they haven't been constrained in how they use the house.

As children and parents get older, the guest bedroom on the main floor, now occupied only when Caroline's parents come to visit, will become an adaptable space that can provide parents or teenagers with privacy. If Caroline and Peter grow old

The stair landing is big enough to serve as another play place. The little window offers views from the children's loft.

an inimitable sense of French style, Caroline has personalized the first floor with a painted mural that embraces the doorway (see the photo on p. 120) and displays of dried flowers and wooden Camembert boxes; perfume bottles catch the light in the windows. Her place of her own, with its windows on the floor, has recently become a temporary bedroom—with the mattress on the floor, she and Peter can look out the low windows and see the best views in the house. Even though they

This house offers plenty of evidence of how a family can make its mark. A hand-painted mural is a whimsical and personal addition to the stairway—even the skirt board sprouts grass!

together in this house, the placement of a guest suite on the first floor allows for the possible conversion into a master suite, if there were ever to be issues of mobility.

When you design a house for a family, if you plan to live there for any length of time, it's good to consider who you are today and who you will be as the years pass. Infants grow into teenagers, and teenagers into young adults who eventually move away to start their own lives. The house that at one time needed four bedrooms to accommodate children and the occasional guest can become virtually empty when kids leave for college.

The Not So Big House can be a house for a lifetime, if you think about how the house will age as your family does. The floorplans on p. 122 show a house for a couple—a computer programmer and a violinist—who have three children, ranging in age from seven to infant. The site they chose to build on in Colorado has panoramic views of city lights and mountain tops. Wanting to invest in their future, they determined that the location of the house was primary and so they spent more of their budget on the site than is typical. The house itself would have to be less expensive, with the idea that as time went by they could add to the original structure. We determined to design by level: giving them a finished lower level and first floor, with the opportunity to complete the second level and attic as time and finances allowed. On a flat site, the lower level would be a basement, but the significant sloping character of the site allowed us to put in three bedrooms with full-sized windows, with the result that the finished space feels like anything but a basement.

Why should a window just let in light? In this house, every windowsill is considered a place to display a collection. Here, a colorful row of perfume bottles catches the light and beautifies the view of a deck beyond.

The two youngest children, both girls, share a bedroom, while the older child, a boy, has his own, complete with a child-sized fort under the stairs. Both bedrooms are quite small, measuring only 9 ft. 3 in. wide by 14 ft. long. Built-in bunks, desks, and toy storage allow the rooms to function as much bigger spaces. An outdoor play area on the flat roof of the attached garage (see the lower right floorplan on p. 122) gives the children space to spread out during the good weather.

MAIN LEVEL

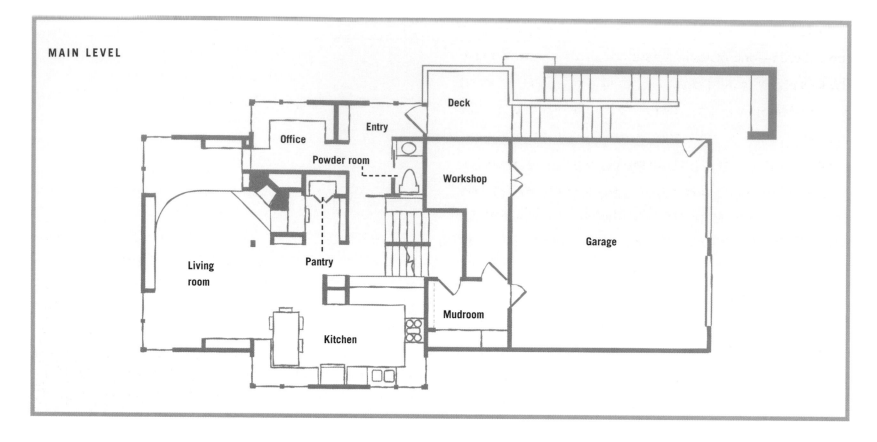

- Deck
- Entry
- Office
- Powder room
- Workshop
- Garage
- Pantry
- Living room
- Mudroom
- Kitchen

LOWER LEVEL

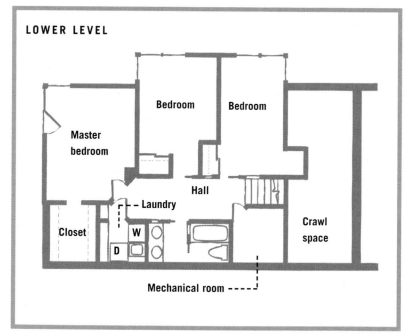

- Bedroom
- Bedroom
- Master bedroom
- Hall
- Laundry
- W
- D
- Closet
- Crawl space
- Mechanical room

UPPER LEVEL

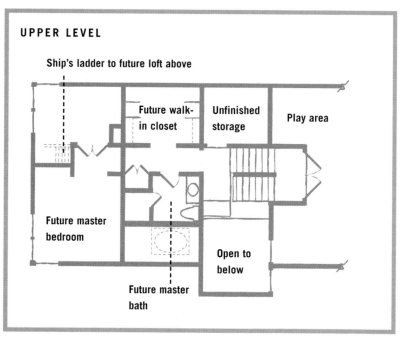

- Ship's ladder to future loft above
- Future walk-in closet
- Unfinished storage
- Play area
- Future master bedroom
- Open to below
- Future master bath

A window in the kitchen allows the parents to keep an eye on the children—one of their biggest concerns was how to give the kids play space in such mountainous terrain. In the future, as their children get older, the couple has the option of enclosing the area above the garage and turning it into the away room, a place for the parents to escape. What is currently the parents' bedroom will eventually become one of the girls' rooms, when the parents complete the upstairs. The walk-in closet off the master bedroom is roughed in for a future bathroom, so that this room can, on occasion, do double duty as a guest bedroom when the daughter moves temporarily into her sister's room. This kind of flexible thinking for the future allows for one less bedroom.

The main level contains the family living areas, as well as an office for the husband, who likes the option of working at home. Upstairs, currently unfinished, there's room for a true couple's realm—with a walk-in closet, bath, and two places of one's own, one adjacent to the master bedroom, and the other in the attic above, accessed by a ship's ladder. This family has built the outlines of their dream. When the house is finished, it will be an expression of the lives they've made together.

It is, of course, impossible to plan for another significant way families can change—when a divorce or a remarriage happens and two families are "blended." Remember the Brady Bunch? ("And then one day this lady met this fellow, They knew that it was much more than a hunch, that this group would somehow form a family…that's the way they became the Brady Bunch.") The most important thing to do when designing for blended families is to give each kid a place of his or her own to

Children's bedrooms can be no bigger than a bunk; this one's tucked under the eaves, with a bookshelf forming the headboard. A drape offers privacy and creates a kid-sized hideaway.

retreat to. Such a space does not need to be large, and a good design solution might be to provide multiple bunk beds (as Robert Brady, an architect, did in the television series), each with a curtain or drape that gives them separation from the larger room. Although an adult might consider this space too small, most children love bunks precisely because of their "cocoon-like" quality, which makes kids feel safe and protected.

In all houses for families—blended or not—it's critical to provide a spectrum of spaces from public to private to allow for all the different kinds of situations that present themselves when you're raising children.

Designing for Kids

When I was designing a house for clients with a five-year-old daughter, the adults both embraced the idea of a place of their own for each of them. Toward the end of construction, Anna, their child, announced that she also wanted such a place. We found it under the stairs. I'll never forget standing there with her parents, seriously considering the design elements of this small place. The parents were seeking my counsel on how it should look. "Have you asked Anna?" I inquired. When we asked her what she wanted, she was very clear. "I see a tiny space with a green door with a round top and a diamond window in it," she announced, as if she were receiving some celestial vision—and that's exactly what she got.

Designing for children is one of the most gratifying aspects of my architectural practice. Kids are an architect's best audience. Not only do they embrace the idiosyncrasies of a design but they also figure out ways to use spaces that even the designer didn't realize could be possible. And they are almost always willing to tell you what they want, either by expressing it, as Anna did, or by their actions.

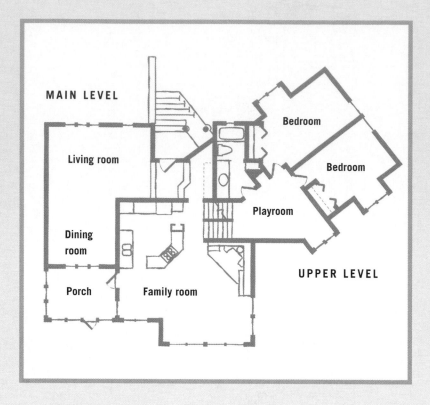

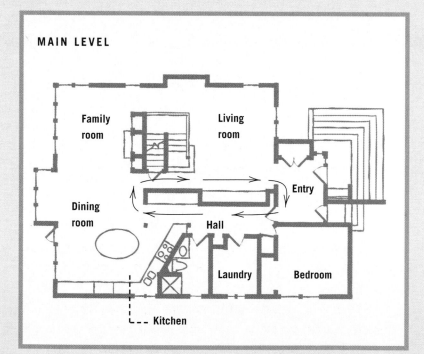

Children are bundles of energy who significantly affect the workability of any house design. Homes that work well for a couple without children may be totally impractical for a family with young kids. Anyone knows that children like to be where the action is. When they are little, they like to be close to their parents, so when I'm designing for a young family, I try to make sure there is a "loop" somewhere in the house—preferably close to the kitchen and family gathering areas, for children to race around without getting in the way of food preparation (see the floorplan at left). This loop adds a kind of planned-for race track that answers some of the challenges of creating a house for families with active kids.

As kids grow older, they still like to be close to the center of adult activity, which can create traffic jams in places of food preparation. By designing places where they can play and simultaneously see what the adults are up to, both the needs of parents and children can be met. In the floorplan above, the stair landing was expanded to become a playroom, a sort of anteroom to the

Kids love spaces that are scaled to fit their size. The desk area is tucked below a play loft, the envy of the neighborhood's younger set.

children's bedrooms. Perched on the landing, the children can keep an eye on mom at all times, without being underfoot.

Kids like places that are kid-scaled. A child's bedroom can really be quite tiny. I've seen successful rooms carved out of kneewall space, with just a bed and a curtain separating it from a play area. Kids also love bunk beds. One of the most successful space-saving solutions for kids' bedrooms is to design multiple bunk beds. Not only are bunk beds like mini-jungle gyms but they also provide smaller spaces by creating a sort of stacked alcove where kids love to play and to sleep.

Remember when you design for children to plan for places that are kid-scaled, places that offer opportunity for play and invention. And watch the way your kids find ways to use spaces to meet their needs—we can all learn from their creativity and flexible thinking.

A remodeling for a retired couple added 500 sq. ft. to their weekend house. It also turned the home into a place where the owners plan to grow old together.

A House for Empty Nesters

When Fred and Marvel, an older couple whose children had left home, determined that their second home would become the house where they would retire, they contacted architect Kelly Davis to help them make it a place where they could grow old together. The original house had been designed in the 1980s by Mike McGuire, an architect with whom Davis had previously been in business. McGuire used the forms of Midwestern farm buildings to give the house a kind of rambling, organic shape. Davis, in planning a 500-sq.-ft. addition, was inspired by the original shape of the house and the farmhouse tradition of growing horizontally as the building responds to the needs of its owners.

The addition converted an existing screened porch into a master suite, and then extended the kitchen, on the opposite

Before

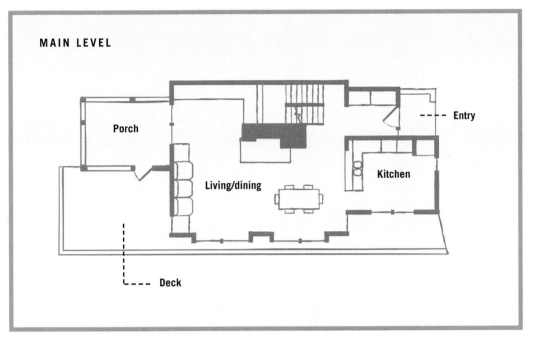

MAIN LEVEL

Porch

Living/dining

Kitchen

Entry

Deck

After

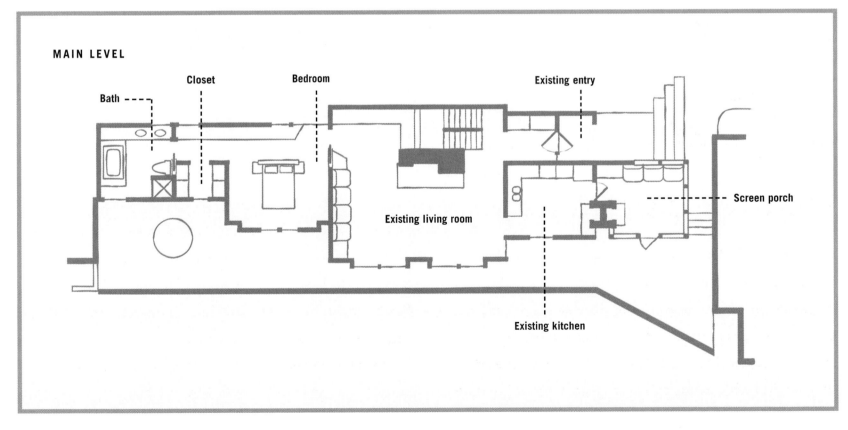

MAIN LEVEL

Bath

Closet

Bedroom

Existing entry

Existing living room

Screen porch

Existing kitchen

end of the house, with a fireplace for cooking and a screened-in porch for warmer months. Essentially, the clients wanted to move downstairs, where their daily life could be centralized around the kitchen, a place where Marvel likes to plan and cook gourmet meals. Davis used the existing palette of materials to make the addition appear seamless: The pine ceiling and plank floor continue now through the bedroom area. A built-in storage system lines the corridor that connects the bedroom with the living area, a space-saving solution that gives Marvel lots more storage and an area for display (see the photo on p. 130).

The couple's concern about aging in the house has been addressed by putting all everyday living functions on one level. What had been the upstairs master suite is now reserved for guests or visiting family. And, thinking ahead, Davis made the

bedroom, bath, and kitchen addition all handicap-accessible by widening doors and being conscious of how a wheelchair could eventually navigate the space.

The house is a striking example of how architecture can provide a backdrop for the client to make a personal statement. From a basket hung from a ceiling rafter to the rugs on the plank floor, the couple's collection of Swedish-American antiques, handmade baskets, and ethnographic art adorn the house. Marvel, a potter, uses the yard as her gallery, placing various glazed forms throughout her gardens.

People can have quite different approaches to designing a house for retirement years. Some, like these empty nesters, recognize the potential for limited mobility and request that the living areas be on one level. I have had clients in this stage of

The owners of this home wanted to surround themselves with the treasures from a lifetime of traveling. A relatively simple living area, adorned architecturally with beams and large windows, becomes a stunning backdrop for their collections of baskets, weavings, and sculptural items.

life who purposefully build homes that require lots of going up and down stairs. Their attitude is that stairs are like built-in exercise machines. If they reach the point where they can't master the steps, then they will plan to move.

My very first clients in my professional career were a 65-year-old woman and her 98-year-old mother. The mother's eyesight was failing, and she used a walker to get around; nevertheless she was remarkably agile for someone of her age. She did have difficulty in the bathroom, because her right arm was weak. She requested a grab bar to the left of the toilet and asked to have the vanity countertop as close to the right side of the toilet as code would allow, so that she could use the edge to push

The addition of the bedroom to the main level integrates seamlessly with the existing house. A small hallway from the bedroom to the bathroom has a lowered ceiling and a built-in dresser, both of which help define the passageway as its own place.

off with her right elbow. Without such specific data about her particular infirmities, I could not have designed a bathroom that would have worked well for her. To have predicted the need for such elements when she was in her 60s would have been impossible.

But what *does* make sense is to employ some sensible strategies that don't cost a lot of money, or make the house "odd" in the eyes of the resale market if this is a concern. When I am designing a house for a couple approaching retirement, I suggest that we make the main level accessible from the outside by no more than one or two steps. Once inside, there should be no interior steps or changes of level other than the stairway to upstairs or downstairs. Designing this main level so that it can be a self-contained living unit allows the house to function in whatever way may be needed in that unpredictable future. Although the couple's realm may initially be upstairs on a second level, a main-level guest bedroom or den can be designed specifically to become the couple's area in the future, if necessary.

There are some other small considerations that can make a difference to the livability of the house as you get older. Making doors 2 ft. 8 in. wide throughout the house allows most wheelchairs sufficient clearance, without making the openings appear so wide that the house starts to take on an institutional look. Using lever door handles rather than knobs makes opening and closing doors easier for those with arthritic fingers and wrists. The addition of a plywood backer behind the drywall around the midsection of the main-level bathroom allows for easy installation of future grab bars, as it becomes clear where they are needed. Locating the laundry on the main

A bed doesn't have to be pushed against a wall. With built-in headboard and side tables, this bed takes center stage and creates a hallway that leads from the bedroom's entrance to the bath.

level, ideally adjacent to the couple's area, is a good idea. And the location of the oven and microwave should be considered so that the user doesn't have to bend down or reach up to take things in and out. Placing counter surfaces close to the refrigerator and ovens is also important so that items can be set down easily as they are unloaded.

A Not So Big House will age with you. You may have to make changes as time goes by, but these changes are easier and ultimately less expensive than trying to attempt to predict the future. Design for who you are today, recognize that there will changes—and make your house something that can grow and adapt as you do, rather than something complete and ready for a future that may never happen.

"Form follows function—that has been misunderstood. Form and function should be one, joined in a spiritual union."
—Frank Lloyd Wright

Every year, our firm has a booth at the local Home and Garden Show. This event is always a good opportunity to talk to people from all walks of life, many of whom dream of building a house. At a recent show, an older man came up to the booth to talk to us about building his dream house. He and his wife had spent at least a decade planning their retirement home. They had purchased the land some time before and had spent years compiling images of houses they liked. The man showed us a collection of articles, many of them about houses our firm had designed over the years. He seemed to be a fan of our work.

It was clear from the way he spoke that his dream house would be expensive: 3,000 sq. ft., with a high level of architectural detail. Unfortunately, and despite his dreams, his budget would afford him only a smaller (2,000 sq. ft. or so) standard builder home. Given the reality of his finances, I told him that the most sensible thing to do would be to find a set of architecturally designed plans (avail-

Dream houses like this one, with 3,600 sq. ft., a complex form, and lots of interior detailing, are budget-breakers for most of us. People often fall in love with a house that is several times more expensive than they can afford.

would have to start with a very simple, easy-to-build shape. As for details, using standard materials creatively would be the way to give the house the character he was seeking.

The basic problem with home-design books and magazines is that there's almost nothing in them that communicates to the public the hard facts about the costs of building a house. If the quality and character of a house are paramount, then there must be an understanding of the impact on cost.

Quality, Quantity, Cost

Building a house, more than any other undertaking, pits our dreams against our realities. When we think about dollars we tend to be very practical. Dreams, by their very nature, are often impractical. The reconciliation of the two is never an

able from a home-plans publication) and work from there. That way he could save on architectural fees, which can run 10% to 15% of construction costs. He called two weeks later, excited about a plan he and his wife had selected. They wanted to discuss the possibility of making a few alterations to it—expanding the kitchen and adding a bedroom. When we met and I saw the plan he had purchased, my heart sank. The plan was, in fact, substantially larger than the original house he'd hoped for, and in its detailing it was a high-style Prairie, with probably $80,000 worth of trim, which represented more than one third of his total budget. I knew the house itself would be at least four times the cost of his budget. (So much for saving architectural fees!)

I felt awful as I explained to him that the house was far beyond his range. If he wanted even a 2,000-sq.-ft. house, we

Building with simple forms and less expensive materials is one way to reconcile our dreams of home with the realities of our budgets.

Making Wish Lists and Reality Lists

To define what features you want in a house, it's helpful to use a couple of tools that architects often employ with their clients. Start by making a wish list. It should include all the dreams and visions you have for your home, even if you know that many of the items are beyond the scope of your budget. Think back through your life to all the houses, rooms, and places that have given you pleasure. Imagine including such places in your own home. Supplement the list with drawings and pictures—and anything else that helps describe your wishes.

Once you have completed this exercise, go through the wish list and identify which of the items are "musts," which are desirable but you could live without if necessary, and which are in the realm of dreams only. Then take the items that are in the must list and describe each more specifically. Now make a list of any items that were not a part of your wish list but are important to include in a list of needs. This is your reality list. The more specific you are, the more likely it is that your house will meet your needs.

Each of these lists is helpful to an architect, or to anyone working with you on the design. Although you must make clear what are dreams only, the two lists help describe not just the quantifiable aspects of your dream home but also the qualities that are important to you. In addition, they may tell you something about your life that you had not anticipated.

Several years ago I was working with a young female attorney, and one of the key elements on her reality list was a greenhouse—a BIG greenhouse. As I worked with her and got to know her better, I realized that the greenhouse she wanted represented a wish, not a reality. It was a wish for free time, and for something that could feed her soul. I made this observation, as tactfully as I could, in one of our meetings. The revelation proved to be correct. Her wish was an expression of her frustration with how busy she was, with no time for herself and no hope of finding any. The size of the greenhouse was simply an indication of the size of her frustration. She wanted something to bring her life back into balance and to reconnect her both literally and figuratively with the earth.

It's hard to see these contradictions ourselves, but they constitute one of the primary reasons that our houses get bigger than we really want or need. We accommodate our wishes, but often these wishes remain only wishes even after the place to realize them is built. If the wish is going to become reality, a change of lifestyle is needed more than a new place. If you can change your lifestyle, then the place for the wished-for activity is a sensible investment. But if you know that you aren't going to change, recognize this and move on. Developing a discrimination for what is a need and what is a wish can allow your house to become a place that has true meaning for you and relevance to the way you live.

Wish List
* I want a house that is small, beautifully designed, & unusual
* I imagine the view to the backyard to be something that you discover as you move through the house, & not immediately apparent.
* The entry process is really important to me. I'd like the main entry we greet guests at, and the entry we come in through on a daily basis to be the same one, or at least both doors arriving into the same space.
* I really like changes of level, but know how much these cost, and so would probably forgo such changes to keep costs down. Ceiling height variety however is very important.

Reality List
Kitchen: Don't need double oven
Design for 2' deep refrig.
Gas range
Built-in pantry
An island, ideally with barstools if there's room
Place for cat food, & cat dishes
Bread making supplies are key
Appliance garage for:
  - bread maker
  - coffee grinder
Ideally maple or cherry cabs.
No handles visible
Small microwave
Place for cookbooks

Dining: No need for formal dining
Table to serve both formal & informal situations
Needs to be very comfort
This is our main 'hang'

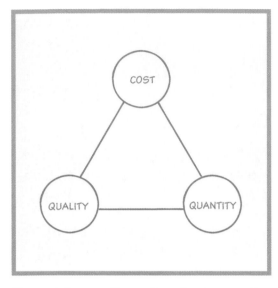

Three variables—quality, quantity, and cost—govern the decision-making process in house design and construction.

easy thing—and yet, in building a house, it's essential that the two come together. People's dreams are frequently two to three times more expensive than the realities of their pocketbook. The challenge is to find a way to bring dreams and realities in line with one another, without making people feel as though they've given up on their dreams.

Whenever I work with a client, I point out the three variables involved in reconciling dreams with realities: quality, quantity, and cost. Cost seems like the most obvious of the three: How much are you willing to spend to accomplish your dream? Often, what people think they can afford increases over the course of the project because they don't want to compromise on their dreams. The budget that at first seemed so absolute rises commensurately.

Quantity also seems like an obvious factor. Some people assume that they need a house of a certain size, because all the houses they've seen and liked are that size. But by going

through the process outlined in earlier chapters, you may find a way to reduce quantity and reallocate your money into higher-quality materials or detailing. For others, quantity is important, and the desire to live in a bigger space is what prompted them to consider building a new house in the first place. If size has nothing to do with your vision, then the quality of the space—the materials or character of the house—can be achieved with the reduction of square footage.

As you think about your own dreams and realities, it's useful to picture quality, quantity, and cost as the three points of a triangle. In designing and building a new house, two of these three variables can remain constant, but the third has to be adjustable. (Most houses are built with the quantity and cost fixed; the variable that has to give is quality.) Whenever I start to work with new clients I try to gauge where they fall on the quality-quantity-cost triangle. Are they the type who will want more space, even if they have to sacrifice quality of materials and execution to get it? Or are they astute observers of detail who will want fine finishes and craftsmanship even if the house has to be smaller so they can afford it? Or are they interested in both the quality and the size they have determined and willing and able to let the cost increase to accommodate both?

For clients who want to maintain both quality and quantity, I start the discussion by making sure they understand that this decision means higher costs. Allowing cost to be the variable offers the greatest flexibility in terms of design and fulfillment of dreams, but it's the rare client who has this option. If any party in the team—client, builder, or architect—is intransigent about the triangle and insists that no one variable can be flexible, then you simply cannot build the house. In this chapter,

In this addition, quality was the one variable the client refused to compromise on. No expense was spared—from elaborate trimwork to custom stained glass—and as a result the cost per square foot was very high.

137

Colonial style houses are so prevalent because their form is very simple and therefore economical to build. They enclose a maximum of square footage with a minimum of surface area.

we'll look at a variety of projects, each of which illustrates the choices the clients have been willing to make in order to reconcile dreams with realities.

The Economical House

A realtor couple I know, who often work with wealthy clients, contacted me because they wanted to build their own home. Because they were so well versed in new homes, they knew that the houses they liked best were architecturally designed. While they were familiar with the high-end houses that our firm had designed, their own budgets dictated something that would be much more economical. As far as clients go, these two were pretty savvy—knowledgeable about how the detail and quality of a space can make it special but aware that their resources would preclude them from even considering many of the high-end homes they sold to other people.

There are certain decisions you can make at the beginning of the process to keep costs down. The first and most important is to keep the form or shape of the house square or rectangular. A complex shape costs a considerable amount more because there is more surface area per square foot of interior space. The outer "skin" of a building is typically the most expensive component of the house. Not only do exterior materials cost a significant amount, but making these materials keep the weather out is a significant undertaking, filled with complexity; and this of course costs money.

Have you ever wondered why there are so many Colonial-style houses built around the country? What is it about this form that is so appealing? The shape is very simple, and in terms of getting the most "bang for your buck," it encloses the most space for the least amount of money. In addition, the floors are typically 9 ft. from floor to floor, meaning that the house can be framed easily using standard 8-ft. studs and 10-in. to 12-in. floor joists (see the sidebar on pp. 140-141). Typically, there's a center bearing wall, which makes framing the floor simple, and there are no odd angles or vaulted ceilings. Every square foot of potential space is used for living area. When someone is looking for a way to make their dollars stretch the farthest, it's impossible to ignore the benefits of keeping the form simple. In general, the fewer corners you have in the exterior perimeter, the less expensive the house will be.

My clients were willing to start with a rectangular shape. But to avoid a boxlike feel, I planned for a "bump-out" in the stairwell, which would give the interior a dramatic, light-filled stairway as well as provide some visual relief to the exterior. This detail has since become a focal point of the house. The placement of the porch and the garage, flanking either side of the house, was intended to extend the house and to increase

The couple who built this house had a fixed budget. The primary money-saving decision they made was to minimize exterior construction costs so they could spend more on the interior detailing. The house has a very simple rectangular form, with a garage and a screened porch on either side.

A Construction Primer

The construction trades have developed a series of conventions that dictate which materials to use and the techniques for using them. These conventions are not absolute rules but rather indicate the methods builders have developed to achieve the best results with a minimum amount of decisions made in the field. Adhering to these conventions won't guarantee a minimum price, but it will help keep the cost down.

To understand this concept better, let's look at some of the component parts that go into building a house. The fewer changes made to the original size and shape of these components, the more money can be saved.

CEILING HEIGHT

The convention is 8-ft. or 9-ft. ceilings, although there's currently an increased use of the 10-ft. ceiling since materials are being made available that allow easier assembly of the

Manufactured and pre-engineered floor trusses, an alternative to standard-dimension lumber joists, allow for longer unsupported spans. Ductwork and wiring can be laced between and through the trusses.

10-ft. wall. The most common wall-finish material, drywall, is also readily available in sizes to fit these wall heights.

To build an 8-ft. ceiling, the most typical construction method is to use a "pre-cut" wall stud of 92⅝ in. This dimension, used with one floor plate below and two horizontal plates above, results in a wall height of 8 ft., after allowing for floor and ceiling finishes. Pre-cut studs are also available for 9-ft. ceilings. A common mistake made by the inexperienced is to order 8-ft. studs, which result in an 8-ft. 4-in. ceiling when you add in the other necessary framing members. Although the added ceiling height can be a benefit, gypsum board is made for the pre-cut 8-ft. length, making the drywall process both more labor-intensive and expensive.

FLOOR JOISTS

The most common size floor joist used today is the 2x10. Large floor areas uninterrupted by columns or supporting walls require a floor structure that goes beyond the capabilities of the conventional 2x10 floor joist. The 2x10 board, which is actually 1½ in. by 9¼ in., has a maximum span of about 15 ft. 6 in. when installed at the conventional 16 in. on center. In the past 20 years, more options have become available to achieve longer spans, such as manufactured floor joists and pre-engineered floor trusses (see the photo at left). These members are manufactured in depths ranging from typical joist sizes up to 24 in. or more and are available in almost all market areas. But, in general, the longer the clear, unsupported span, the more you pay.

FOUNDATION WALLS

Foundation walls, which are built into the ground and support all the weight of the house, are typically made of concrete or concrete block. The forms into which the concrete is poured are made of plywood or steel panels. As might be expected, multiple corner offsets, changes in elevation, and curved forms require more work and consequently cost more. In regions where concrete block is used for basement walls, it is typical to use a 12-in. block. This unit actually measures 11⅝ in. thick, 15⅝ in. long, and 7⅝ in. high. Including the mortar joints, it lays up in the wall as 16 in. long and 8 in. high. In some foundations that are not part of a basement (such as beneath a garage), 8-in. (7⅝-in.) or 10-in. (9⅝-in.) thick block is used.

ROOF FRAMING

Up until the 1960s most roofs were framed up one board at a time, a process referred to in the trade as hand framing. Although some builders still prefer this method of building a roof, this process is being replaced more and more by the use of roof trusses, which are prefabricated at a factory and delivered to the job site ready for installation (see the photo at right). These trusses can easily accomplish spans of 30 ft. or more and can be made in a wide variety of configurations. Because roof trusses are typically fabricated using computerized equipment to figure out the most efficient method of construction, almost any roof form that doesn't have living space within it can be made to order at much lower cost and with much greater speed than if the roof were hand-framed.

It is because of the advent of these factory-made trusses that we see so many more varied roof forms today than we did even a decade ago. Unfortunately, they are not always designed to be aesthetically pleasing. They are simply configured to cover the floor space below, which can result in some pretty odd-looking forms.

There is one form of truss that's popular today, called the "scissor" truss, that allows a vaulted ceiling inside. Another is the "room-in-the-roof" truss, or storage truss, which allows the use of some of the space inside the roof area but is more expensive than one without this option.

Before roof trusses became the norm and hand framing was the only option for roof construction, having space in the

Factory-fabricated roof trusses have made framing a roof much easier and faster, but they have also eliminated attic space in the majority of new homes.

roof that could be used for living space was a cost-saving option. Many people still have a great love for the look of the Cape Cod cottage, with its dormers bringing light into this roof space. But today, because of the gravitation to roof trusses as the norm, the roof form of the Cape Cod cottage no longer provides the cheap space option that it used to. As a result, people who prefer a smaller-scale, more cottage-like look can end up spending more money for a house that looks smaller and is indeed more compact.

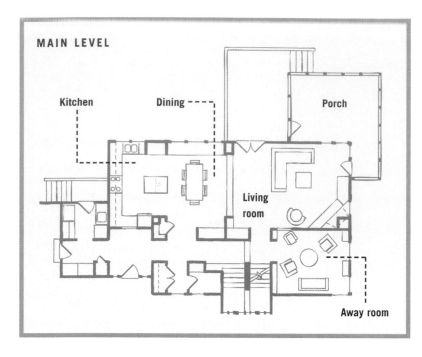

MAIN LEVEL

Kitchen   Dining   Porch

Living room

Away room

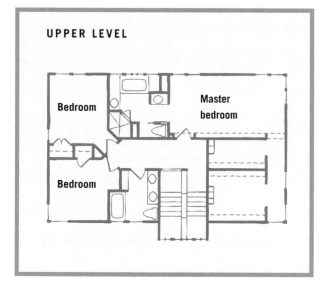

UPPER LEVEL

Bedroom   Master bedroom

Bedroom

The kitchen features standard builder materials like plastic laminate and flush-panel cabinets. With thoughtful design, these elements are brought together into an artful composition that transcends their humble nature.

the sense of its size. If necessary, the porch could have been built at a later time, if the bids had come in too high. When you're working with a tight budget, it's useful to identify sections of the house that can be eliminated or built later.

As for the quantity of the space, the couple were very willing to consider many of the Not So Big concepts, including a com-bined dining and living area and an away room (see the top floorplan at left). So, by reducing the quantity of the space by at least 500 sq. ft., more of their budget could go to the char-acter of the house. With its low-slung hipped roof and wide eaves, the house looks substantially bigger than its 2,100 sq. ft. To save additional dollars, a lower grade of cedar was used in an artful way on the exterior for trim and siding.

The one variable the clients were not willing to compromise on was character—or the quality of the interior space. The expense of a material doesn't always ensure that it's going to lend a house a sense of quality. If the material isn't used artfully, it's simply money down the drain. For this couple, quality was not connected with high-end materials but in how the materials were used. They were interested in using standard building materials, in standard sizes (like 8-ft. studs and off-the-shelf cabinets), which allowed them to save a substantial amount of money. By using economical materials in innovative ways, we were able to make the house more interesting architecturally.

In the kitchen, standard maple cabinets with a very simple design are integrated with a plastic-laminate countertop (see the photo on the facing page). Inexpensive tiles are used as a backsplash. Although all these materials could readily be found in any run-of-the-mill builder's house, the contemporary styling makes the house look infinitely more appealing. In the dining/living areas, alcoves, which are made by lowered soffits and interior wing walls, not by the exterior form, add visual interest and save money. The living area is distinguished from the dining area by two steps down, which enlivens the space and saves its long narrow configuration from feeling like a bowling alley (see the photo below). An away room adjacent to the living area doubles as an office and reading area.

Combining the kitchen, dining, and living area and leaving out the formal spaces reduced the square footage by 500 sq. ft., allowing the homeowners to spend more on interior detailing. A wood trim line marks the lowered soffit and continues around the perimeter of the interior walls.

The living room is two steps down from the adjacent dining area, which increases the ceiling height in this part of the house. Upper transom windows bounce light into the room from the bottom of the soffit.

The clients liked the use of an interior trim line, which is a feature of many of the older Arts and Crafts homes in the city where they live. This trim line became the primary interior detail, continuing through every space in the house along the upper soffit or above the windows. It is the principal feature that distinguishes this house from standard builder construction. During the construction process the clients thought they might save a little by omitting the trim on the upper level.

But they quickly discovered that without this detail the bedrooms lost the unique character of the main level, so they determined to put the additional $500 for the trim back into the budget. It was money well spent: The consistency of the trim line lends the house an elegance and makes it look like a more expensive home.

The addition of corner windows in the bedrooms helps distinguish each space, as shown in the photo below. A striking

The bedrooms feature corner windows, which help make the rooms seem bigger, and the same trim line from downstairs. This detail unifies the two floors and transforms these simple bedrooms into spaces with greater personality and style.

The mirror in the master bathroom extends right up to the soffit and over to the exterior wall, which gives the illusion of a room double the size, with twice as many windows. Glass block, which comes down to the tub, lets in light but obscures the view.

glass-block triptych window on the stair landing enlivens both upstairs and downstairs. The two bathrooms are small, but the careful consideration of standard fixtures, cultured-marble countertops, glass block, and a well-placed mirror makes them seem bigger and more elegant (see the photo on p. 145).

This house, which is in the suburbs, is considerably smaller and less expensive than its neighbors. But by sacrificing only square footage and complexity of form, the owners have built a Not So Big House at a not so big price.

The Site and Your Budget

One of the first decisions to make when designing and building a new home is to determine how much of your budget will go to the site and how much to the design and construction.

A glass-block triptych on the stair landing brings light to both the upstairs and the downstairs. The clear blocks allow a sense of the view, while also providing some privacy for the residents.

The site you choose will significantly affect your budget. The lot that this house was built on slopes steeply from right to left and sold for less than most of its neighbors. The house was designed for the site and nestles perfectly into the slope.

While any realtor will stress the importance of "location, location, location," the fact remains that if you're building for the long term, you may choose to build in an area that has slightly less financial security, in terms of resale, but might have features that are desirable to you. For example, a good location for resale, such as an upscale suburb of new homes, will cost more money than a piece of land in an established neighborhood of small, postwar houses. A good rule of thumb is that a quarter to a third of an entire budget goes to lot cost and the rest to design and construction. If you want a highly detailed house on a limited budget, you might consider finding a piece of land that is less expensive so you can spend more per square foot on the house's construction. A banker can be a good source of advice on what the neighborhood you're considering can support in terms of construction cost.

Sometimes odd-shaped lots can be found that are less expensive, simply because people can't figure out or find a plan to fit them. In fact, nine times out of ten, this kind of lot will bring people into an architect's office as a last resort. From an architect's standpoint, a site that appears impossible can often lead to the most inspiring and ultimately exciting house design. The constraints of budget and of site peculiarities can create a very unique house. The house shown in the bottom photo on the facing page presented an interesting challenge: a site that slopes steeply from right to left. The doctor couple who approached our office came only because there was no plan on the market that could gracefully fit into this unusual piece of property. The solution was to make the house split-level, with the garage slightly more than half a level down from the main living area.

House Orientation

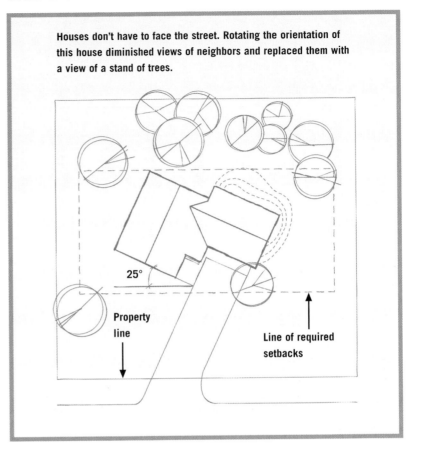

Houses don't have to face the street. Rotating the orientation of this house diminished views of neighbors and replaced them with a view of a stand of trees.

25°

Property line

Line of required setbacks

Taking advantage of the site features can make a home much more interesting, often without any additional expense. The site plan above shows a house our firm designed for a single father and his three children. The client's budget was extremely limited, and the site he found to build on was not particularly distinguished: The neighboring houses were very close and very plain. But the lot had a few nice trees and a location convenient to the client's office and the children's school. A simple solution we came up with was to rotate the orientation of the house by 25°, turning it so that it didn't look directly into its neighbor's windows. This solution cost no more money, and it improved the quality of life and views within the house.

A steeply sloped site can transform what would normally be the basement into desirable living space. This site slopes 9 ft. from the front entry to the back door. Windows in the lower level are low to the ground and offer views that are as appealing as those on the main and upper levels.

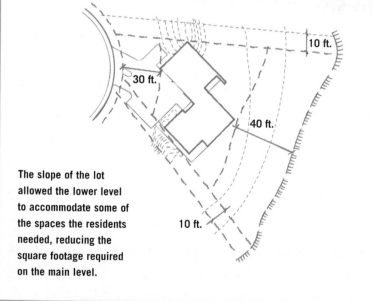

10 ft.

30 ft.

40 ft.

10 ft.

The slope of the lot allowed the lower level to accommodate some of the spaces the residents needed, reducing the square footage required on the main level.

In colder climates, a sloping piece of land can provide a distinct financial advantage when you're building Not So Big. Houses in cold climates require frost footings, which on a flat piece of land would create a basement level. If you have to have frost footings, it doesn't cost too much more to make this basement level another story of living space. A piece of land with a drop of 6 ft. to 10 ft. from front to back will lend itself to a "walk-out" plan, which allows a door from the lower level to open directly to the backyard. If you don't want this lower level to feel like a basement, you'll need plenty of windows, with their sills no more than 2 ft. 6 in. off the floor to keep you connected to a view of the ground beyond. This kind of plan allows you to reduce the square footage of the main and upper levels by redistributing living space to the lower floor. In the overall cost per square foot, this strategy can save you as much as a third of the cost of the house. The area is already there, so the cost of finishing it is significantly less than the cost of building an upper level from scratch.

The same strategy on a flat site will also save money. A "split entry" is the least expensive house you can build in a cold climate, where in some really cold areas frost footings are required to extend 4 ft. below ground. A split entry means that you enter the house halfway between the main level and the lower level, as shown in the drawing at right. Typically in such a house, the main living areas are upstairs and the bedrooms are downstairs. Without adding any more foundation than is required for frost-footing depth, you have a comfortable living level. Although windows cannot be as low to the floor, for someone with a limited budget this model buys the most space for the least money.

The site, perhaps more than any other factor, affects the quantity, quality, and cost of your house. The quality of a Not So Big House depends on making maximum use of every single opportunity offered by the site. Designing Not So Big means trading quantity of space for quality—and this idea should inform the lot you choose to build on.

The way the Not So Big House interacts with its site is symbiotic, but sometimes the features offered by a site aren't immediately evident. A client of mine was considering two lots on a city lake. The more expensive lot had unobstructed views to

Split-Entry House

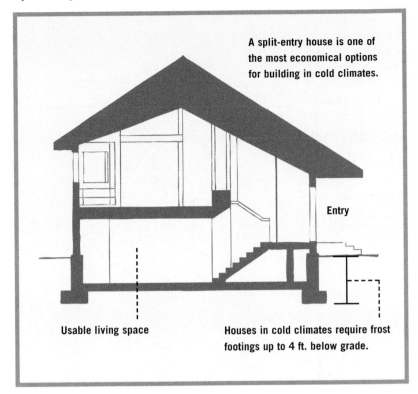

A split-entry house is one of the most economical options for building in cold climates.

Entry

Usable living space

Houses in cold climates require frost footings up to 4 ft. below grade.

the lake and to the houses beyond. The less expensive lot had no views because of the dense foliage. By trimming some of the lower branches, the view to the lake was opened but the nearby houses were still obscured. The client bought the less expensive lot, which turned out to be the most desirable.

Often the beauty of a piece of land is what inspires people to build a house worthy of that land. So when you're looking for a lot it's important to consider special features like long views, the presence of water, and distinctive trees and rock formations, which will ultimately affect the livability of the house. Most important is daylight. The pattern of the sun's movement will not only affect the orientation of the house but also offer perhaps the cheapest form of interior decoration: sunlight. The smaller the house the more profound the effect of the sun upon

This house was built for an owner who was willing to sacrifice square footage for interesting interior details.

it. Good resources for this topic include the books *Sun, Wind, and Light: Architectural Design Strategies* by G. Z. Brown and V. Cartwright (John Wiley and Sons, 1985) and *Passive Solar Energy* by Bruce Anderson and Malcolm Wells (Brick House Publishing, 1994).

The Middle Ground

Between the most economical of houses and the most expensive exists a broad range of possibilities, each again connected to one aspect of the quality-quantity-cost triangle. By increasing size, you increase cost; by increasing the level of detail, you also increase cost. The house featured in this section employs many of the principles of keeping cost down by using a simple form and structure, but it expands on the idea of quality of space and the craft of the details to become, as the client requested, "a little jewel."

The client, a church organist and choir director who teaches music, wanted a home where he could display various treasures from his travels as well as have space for a home pipe organ. He requested a bedroom that felt like a tree house, a screen porch, and a small deck off the master bedroom. From the kitchen, he wanted to be able to see the outside, the fireplace, and any guests he might be entertaining. Because he had traveled extensively in Asia, he knew he wanted the house to have a Japanese aesthetic. As for the size of the house, he needed at least 1,800 sq. ft., and he was willing to sacrifice any extra square footage to make the house interesting inside.

The site presented a few challenges: It is located on a busy street and slopes down to a marsh. So what would tradition-

The form of the house is a cube, a very simple and economical shape to build. A screened porch located above the garage extends the cube to the left. There are few windows on the front of the house because it faces a busy street.

ly be the front of the house needed to present a more private face, while the back of the house could open up for views. Remember, when you build deep frost footings, you get the chance to add a lower level that would just be a basement on a flat site. For architect Kelly Davis, the relatively tight budget, along with the site considerations, inspired a simple cube for the house form. While the client had originally specified wood siding, Davis was able to convince him that stucco would, ultimately, be a better choice for the exterior even though it would add $5,000 to the cost of the house. The maintenance of the wood exterior, especially on a three-level house, would also cost money. Wood requires frequent staining or painting, while stucco will last for decades without attention. The client and

architect determined that stucco would be easier and more cost-effective to maintain.

The architect's goal in designing the house was to take the very simple cube and give it as much visual interest as possible. This was achieved primarily through interior detailing. With simplicity as the guiding principle, Davis used a limited amount of wood trim to achieve a striking effect. Horizontal lines, valances, and window trim enliven the living areas. Lowered soffits carry ductwork to the upper floor and also provide varied ceiling heights, which are emphasized by lighting along the edge of the soffit. Niches for various treasures create

The back of the house opens up, taking full advantage of the sloped site to create a beautiful lower level that is filled with light and views.

Simplicity is this house's guiding design principle. The living area integrates carefully considered details, such as a trim line and a lowered ceiling along the wall between this room and the foyer, which marks the path to the porch.

interest on every level of the house. The grandfather clock, which has been in the client's family for 100 years, needed a special place. Davis carved an area out of the dropped soffit, rather than just make the ceiling height of the entire area taller. This creates a special alcove just for the clock—and the contrast of the two ceiling heights is striking.

In keeping with Not So Big precepts, Davis employed a number of visual tricks to make certain areas in the house appear bigger than they really are. The entry, which is between the main and lower level, measures only 6 ft. by 8 ft. (see the photo on p. 154). Open stair risers expand the sense of space; the entry's coat closet doesn't go all the way to the ceiling but

To accommodate a tall grandfather clock, the architect carved a niche up into the joist space rather than raising the ceiling height of the entire main level.

Open stair risers offer filtered views both up and down.
A small house like this one benefits from views connecting one
level to another, which makes it seem significantly bigger.

transforms into a display shelf, which is another way to make the entry seem larger. The alcove in the entry is a Japanese idea, a version of the *tokonoma*, which typically displays some sort off seasonal flower arrangement.

Because the house was designed for one person, issues of privacy were not important. So the house is quite open on each of its three levels. The main level uses Not So Big strategies, including a shared living and dining area, which is open to the kitchen. The dining area is distinguished by a two-story ceiling, which is opened up by two levels of windows (see the photo on p. 156). A two-story space is equivalent in cost to almost double the square footage of the area—in other words if the opening had been filled with floor and made into an upper-level room the cost would have been only slightly more. Thus, the cost per square foot of the entire house would have been lower. This client chose to spend money on drama rather than more living space. Although the main living space is relatively small (800 sq. ft.), in the summer months it's almost doubled with the addition of both a porch and a deck, which cover the garage below.

Upstairs, the master bedroom looks out over the dining area. A small study alcove, flooded with light from a large window that looks out to the street, is at the halfway point between the main and upper levels, almost like a big stair landing. The deck the client requested is just off the bedroom. Details enliven every area in the upper level, including the bathroom. A towel bar seems to be an extension of the trim line (see the bottom photo on p. 157); the mirror extends only halfway up the wall, allowing for windows to let in natural light while obscuring views to the busy street. The angle of the mirror allows the

MAIN LEVEL

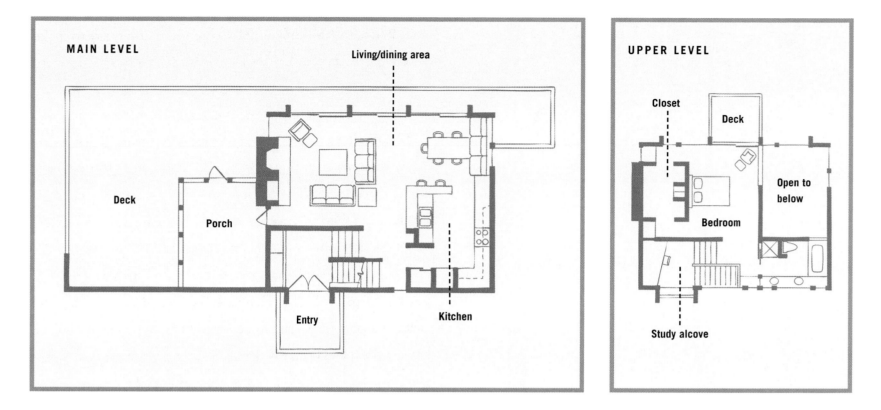

Living/dining area

Deck

Porch

Entry

Kitchen

UPPER LEVEL

Closet

Deck

Open to below

Bedroom

Study alcove

BUILDING SECTION

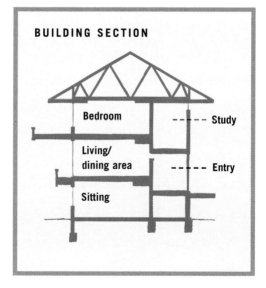

Bedroom — Study

Living/ dining area — Entry

Sitting

LOWER LEVEL

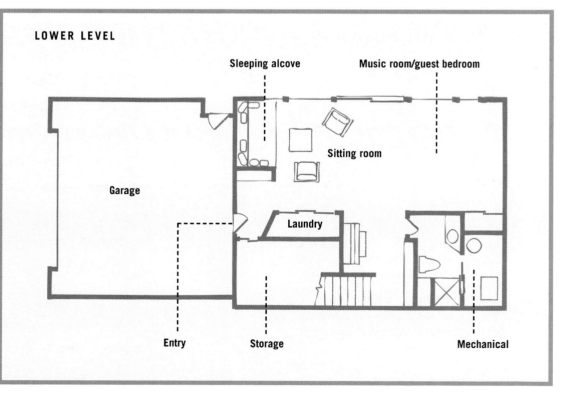

Sleeping alcove

Music room/guest bedroom

Sitting room

Garage

Laundry

Entry

Storage

Mechanical

A two-story ceiling in the dining area creates real dramatic interest on the main level.

The bedroom features a continuous band of maple trim, which aligns with the ceiling of the adjacent bathroom. Niches displaying treasures from the owner's travels are included upstairs and down.

same amount of reflection as would a mirror that goes to the ceiling (see the top left photo on p. 158).

The lower level of the house has become the music room, complete with home pipe organ. A built-in couch doubles as another bed, which the client uses whenever guests come to stay, allowing them the use of the master bedroom. The innovative details continue on this lower level, turning what might have been basement-like space into an extended living area. The client wanted an interesting floor but did not want to spend extra money on it. Exposed-aggregate floors are an economical finish for the lower-level floor. Because this level needed a concrete slab anyway, it cost only an extra dollar per square foot to use exposed aggregate for the finished floor.

Less expensive than most bathroom accessories, these custom-designed towel bars integrate perfectly with the aesthetics of the house.

High windows fill the bathroom with light. The mirror is designed to accommodate the windows and is set at an angle to reflect a greater area.

A lowered ceiling creates a special alcove for a built-in couch on the lower level. The couch doubles as a bed when visitors stay overnight.

The owner of the house is an organist, and the guest bedroom on the lower level doubles as a music room.

Wood dividers inset into the floor give it a more finished look and help limit any cracking that may occur with time (see the photo above).

The budget for this house was about 15% higher per square foot than for the house featured on pp. 138-146. The accumulation of so many special details gives this house a unique personality. Details were considered from the very beginning of

The finishing details are the most common items that can increase the cost per square foot in a new home. The faux finish on the walls of this room cost considerably more than a can of paint.

the design process, and they became the top priority. The client chose to purchase detail over complexity of form, and quality over quantity.

The most common items that can increase the cost per square foot of a new home are materials, fixtures, and finishes. For example, granite countertops, a hand-blown-glass light fixture, a whirlpool-tub faucet, a faux finish on a wall, imported wallpaper, and marble floors can each single-handedly break a budget. But, as shown in the house just profiled, good design can transform simple materials like concrete floors and laminate countertops. In architecturally designed homes, you don't need to rely on expensive materials, fixtures, and finishes to give the house its personality. What affects the cost is the quantity of whatever material is being used, as well as the

Extensive use of interior trimwork adds to the cost of a home. In this interior, the trim covers every edge—there isn't a single drywalled corner. A design like this can only be fully realized by skilled artisans.

craftsmanship with which it is executed. Wood trim, used lavishly (as shown in the photo above), can add a substantial amount to the cost of the house, as can the fee for the high-quality finish carpenter who installs it. If the house for the music teacher had a similar amount of wood trim, the cost of the house might have risen by another 10%.

All wood—from pine to Brazilian cherry—is expensive. Some woods are also nonrenewable, such as hardwoods from tropical forests. Wood used on a broad surface, such as a ceiling, can also significantly affect the cost. And if you add an intricate coffered ceiling, the price is two to three times more than its flat-wood-surface counterpart. Similarly, a soaring ceiling can create real architectural interest, but you pay a premium for it.

Using the form of the roof as a vaulted ceiling costs more than the standard flat ceiling with a truss above it. The reason

A wood ceiling adds warmth to a room, but it also adds expense. The cost of putting wood on a ceiling is roughly equivalent to putting wood on the floor.

A two-story room is a wonderful space for entertaining, but its height makes it almost twice the price of its single-story equivalent.

A coffered ceiling is more expensive than a plain wood ceiling. There's more wood, and it requires significantly more craftsmanship to install.

for this is that any angle or curve simply costs more to finish and requires greater labor and skill than a flat surface. In short, when you deviate from a square box the price automatically goes up. This is why a simple builder house is usually less expensive. When you build a house that has special detailing you must assume that it will cost more, which is another reason to consider reducing square footage so that those special details are where the budget goes.

Exterior finishes can also affect the cost—and again the rule of thumb is that both quality of material and quality of craftsmanship cost money. In the Prairie-style house shown on p. 164, the exterior finishing looks expensive. But by using corner boards, or vertical pieces of trim at each corner of the house, a significant amount of money is saved. That's because the carpenter doesn't have to miter the edges of each piece of siding—a painstaking and expensive process. Although it has

Angles and curves can be beautiful to look at, but they are expensive to create. The curved ceiling that arches over the doorway to a deck looks effortless, but it belies the effort required to make it look so. The labor involved translates to increased cost.

Exterior finishing can figure prominently in a budget, but there are ways to reduce costs. The siding on this Prairie-style house butts up against corner boards at each corner of the house; without the corner boards, each piece of siding would have to be mitered and aligned perfectly with the siding on the adjacent surface.

This house, which, features siding with mitered corners, custom-colored windows, a cedar roof, and a brick base, is considerably more expensive than the one on the facing page, although both are at the high end of the residential market.

a similar aesthetic, the house shown above has a significantly more expensive exterior. The brick, while it is a durable building material, costs substantially more than wood siding; the custom color on the aluminum-clad windows adds to the price; and the wood shingles on the roof are typically five times the cost of a standard asphalt roof.

There are many less expensive alternatives to wood siding, such as steel, aluminum, and vinyl. And all of these products boast low maintenance. But the human eye is hard to fool, so a "fake" product has to be an extremely good replica of the natural product or it will leave the impression of being fake. That's

Four materials meet artfully on a house's exterior: tongue-in-groove redwood, lap siding, and Coronado stone (a fake stone product), topped with a concrete cap.

Increasing the ceiling height in this kitchen and dining area from 8 ft. to 9 ft. led to the inclusion of transom windows above the door and main windows. A change in stud length often has such ramifications throughout the house, which can add substantially to the cost.

a high price to pay. The only synthetic products I use are fake-stone products made of concrete, which can truly fool both the eye and the hand (see the bottom photo on p. 165).

Just as on the interior, angles and curves on the exterior cost money too. Every time you turn a corner or bend a wall, it requires a great deal more craftsmanship and precision by the builder or carpenter. The consequences of what may look like a simple angle in plan will ripple throughout the house. Floor-plans that look interesting on paper can in reality be extremely expensive to build.

Builders often encourage people to increase ceiling height from 8 ft. to 9 ft., telling them that the cost of the studs is only slightly more expensive. But the reality is that the increase in height mandates the addition of other products, such as transom windows, more cabinetry, and more trim to make the height look and feel right (see the photo above).

The High End

If cost is the adjustable parameter on your quality-quantity-cost triangle, then the potential to add character and detail to a house is limitless. The house shown below and on the following pages was designed by Michaela Mahady and built for the television series, *Hometime*. By most people's standards, it is not a small house. However, it does feature many of the Not So Big ideas on its main and upper levels, including a combined kitchen, dining, and living area and an away room (see the floorplans on p. 168).

The floorplans show the house's complexity immediately: If you count the number of corners, it's a pretty good indication of how expensive such a house would be to build. The curved roof form, multiple gables, unusually shaped windows, and stone terrace are all indicative of a very expensive structure. Although this house is significantly larger than any that's been shown so far, it is almost twice as expensive per square foot as the first house shown in this chapter. If the same level of detail were applied to a smaller amount of space, the cost per square foot would be even higher.

This home is much loved for its storybook charm, which comes from some expensive features, such as a curved roof, many dormers, custom-curved windows, and a stone base and chimney.

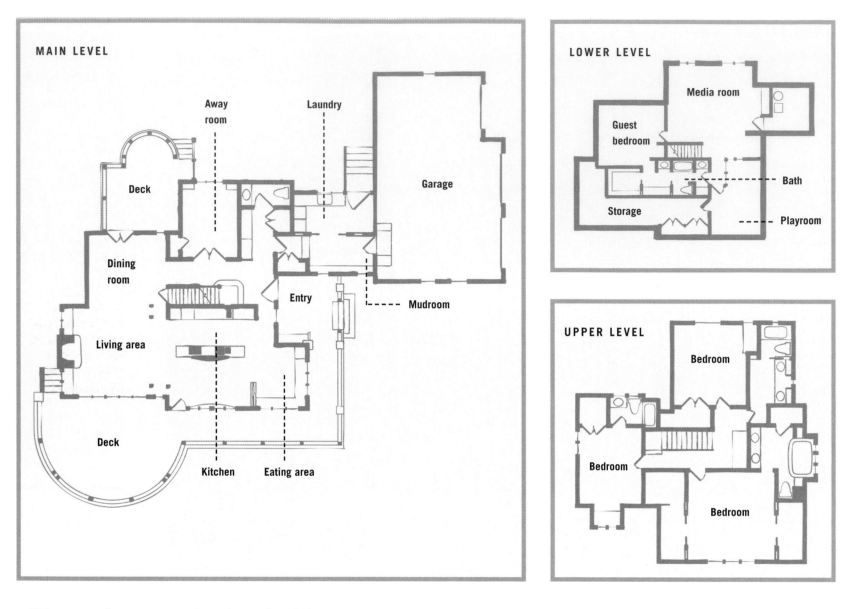

MAIN LEVEL

Away room

Laundry

Deck

Garage

Dining room

Entry

Mudroom

Living area

Deck

Kitchen

Eating area

LOWER LEVEL

Media room

Guest bedroom

Bath

Storage

Playroom

UPPER LEVEL

Bedroom

Bedroom

Bedroom

When you flare out a roof, a plywood web has to be added to the bottom of every roof truss to create the curved form before the roof sheathing is nailed on. And because the slope of the roof has changed, additional flashing and roof membrane have to be installed below the shingles to ensure that the roof won't leak. Every time you add a dormer to a house, you significantly complicate the roof framing, although dormers clearly add a lot of personality to the house. Complexity costs money.

In a house where we're trying to keep costs down, my colleagues and I always use standard windows. The house shown here has windows that are curved and nonstandard in size, as well as upper transom windows used liberally on the main level. Again, these windows give the house a great deal of its personality—but simplifying this element alone could save several thousand dollars. The fieldstone terrace acts as a plinth on which the house is set; although stone is an inexpensive raw material, it takes a lot of labor to set it and, thus, becomes one of the most expensive building materials. If the stonework had covered the foundation alone rather than extending out to make a terrace, less stonework would have been required (and less additional cost). Although the terrace appeals to the eye and adds wonderful exterior space, it essentially adds another expensive foundation wall.

Every detail of this house is beautiful, such as this light fixture set into an arched frame between two symmetrical windows. Such details have to be thought out and planned long before the construction process begins.

From the maple woodwork in the kitchen to the fieldstone hearth beyond, the interior of this house is filled with high-end detailing.

Even the bathrooms feature woodwork throughout. Here, wood wainscoting lines the nook for the toilet and the tub surround. It lends an old-fashioned flair, but the details are luxuriously contemporary.

Special details like the surrounding panels for the exterior lamps, the brackets, the different colors of siding, trim, and shingles all take time and craftsmanship to apply. Inside, everything is custom-designed and detailed to the highest degree—from the kitchen cabinets to the granite and Corian countertops to the top-of-the-line appliances and the lavish use of trim. The detail continues even in more private and utility areas, like the bathroom. Even the stairs and the French doors into the away room have become works of art. In 1997 dollars, this house cost $775,500 to build, with 4,400 sq. ft. of finished space, which translates to $176 per square foot. (Over the last decade, prices have risen approximately 5% per year.)

The clients for the Prairie-inspired house shown at left on p. 172 requested a dramatic two-story living area where they could also feel cozy. Because budget was not a major constraint, I was able to come up with a dramatic solution that required some structural hijinks as well as a significant amount of glass and trim. Essentially, we created shelter around activity by "floating" the second story over the first, through structural beams that transfer the load to the mullion between the win-dows on the main level. The beauty of the form that results is very appealing, but it is only an option when there are dollars available for such complexity.

Architect Joseph Metzler created the high-style Prairie kitchen and dining area addition shown at right on p. 172 for an Arts and Crafts aficionado. It is an example of a small addi-tion that was very expensive to complete. While the original house features simpler Arts and Crafts detailing, the addition is

The stair railing goes beyond function to become sculpture; art-glass doors to the away room echo its lines. Together, these two elements create their own composition of light and line that is delightful to look at.

This room appears deceptively simple, yet it required enormous effort to make it look so. To make the beams that support the second-level window wall align perfectly with the mullions between the picture windows below, every detail had to be planned precisely in the early phases of the design process.

highly decorated with trim, stained glass, and built-in cabinetry. Every material used is custom-crafted and top of the line, from the green-slate countertops to the custom light fixtures. Even the copper sinks were specially made. The walls are handglazed; stereo speakers are hidden in the corner behind a grill. The cost for this kind of detail begins with an architect's fees—

The addition to this home is Not So Big, but very expensive. While it added a combined kitchen/dining area, it also doubled the appraised value of the house.

this kind of precision required more preplanning than a less detailed home, a computer model, and a very specific set of plans for construction. Everyone who works on such a project has to be top-notch, and you'll pay for their skills. In this addition, instead of using expensive furnishings and wallpaper, the architecture itself has been created to become the area's decoration. The cost, which came in close to $500 per square foot in 1997 dollars, almost doubled the appraised value of the house. In the right location, if you have the money available, such an expenditure on architecture can be a rewarding investment.

The greatest challenge in building or remodeling a house lies in making the best use of the dollars available. Building Not So

In this addition, architecture functions also as decoration. Notice the ceiling's trimwork, the lamps, the art-glass transom, the custom cabinets, and faux-finished walls. Details like these can double or triple the cost of the same square footage with a simpler design. Here, cost was of no great concern, so the issue of quality met no barriers.

Big requires a careful evaluation of needs and wishes, based not only on quantities but also, and more important, on qualities of space, light, and character. Our reliance today on the quantifiables of life often makes us settle for security over delight. Keep in mind that the reason you are building your house in the first place is to create a wonderful place to live on a daily basis. The quality-quantity-cost triangle can help you in your decision making, whether you have a tight budget and champagne tastes or an ample budget and a desire for an efficient, elegant environment. If you keep asking yourself what will enhance everyday living as you proceed with the design of your home, you'll ensure that the result makes the best use of the resources available and becomes a place that gives you pleasure every day.

*"We must be the change
we wish to see in the world."*
—Mahatma Gandhi

Throughout this book the case has been made for houses that use less space to give greater quality of life. So far the argument for the Not So Big House has been made based on quality of life for today. But in the design of our houses, we must start to take into consideration their impact on the future. The concepts inherent in building Not So Big are the key to that future: Make better use of raw materials and use less energy to create places of beauty and increase the quality of life in the process. In so doing, we will build the true house of the future.

The house of the future has been imagined by countless architects, designers, and visionaries. In its many variations it has taken the form of a sphere, which boasts the ease of convenient relocation, and a geodesic dome, which was intended to create a new form of construction based on cellular form. The house of the future has appeared in World's Fairs, in roadside attractions, and in national amusement parks. Disneyland proudly displayed Monsanto's "House of

Claude-Nicolas Ledoux, an 18th-century visionary architect, imagined the house of the future as a sphere.

With a circular footprint and a cellular form, a geodesic dome encloses the most area within the least perimeter. While the practical aspects appeal, it doesn't look like home to most of us.

The "House of Tomorrow" looks decidedly space age, evoking futuristic images that are quite alien to our archetypal vision of home.

Tomorrow" in 1957, announcing: "Welcome to the walk-through attraction that provides a glimpse of how you'll be living in the future. You won't find traditional furniture styles or natural materials in the House of the Future. Everything is ultramodern and almost entirely synthetic. It's a demonstration of style and technology." The Monsanto House was on display for only 10 years—both its technology and style out-of-date by 1967.

It seems as though our visions of the house of the future are defined by the technology of the moment: The minute the technology is out-of-date, so too is the style. Remember the earth-sheltered house? The active solar house with its cumbersome solar panels that overwhelm the roofline? The super-insulated house, with a bare minimum of windows? Each of these technologies has influenced the building forms of today, but when a house is designed solely with technology in mind,

Many new technologies prove to be fads and quickly become outmoded. This building is an example of an earth-sheltered house, a form that was very popular in the early to mid-1980s but which proved hard to sell—and to maintain.

Frank Lloyd Wright called his vision of the future the Usonian house. These houses, designed in the 1930s and 1940s, are among this century's most successful visions of the future, perhaps because Wright incorporated people-scaled places with natural materials.

the result is the structural equivalent of a fad. The future, while it holds infinite possibilities, is as changeable as the technology that defines it.

Toward the Not So Big House

One architect working in the early 20th century envisioned the house of the future as something other than a repository for new technology. Frank Lloyd Wright believed that everyone should be able to live in an architect-designed house, each on its own acre of land. Much of his life and work was devoted to

the de-urbanization of America, with the single-family homestead as the basic building block of civilized life. Wright designed a series of houses that were affordable and smaller than the typical house of the day—interestingly enough, promoting the idea even then of eliminating the formal spaces of the house and integrating the kitchen into the primary living space. Wright called these houses Usonian, after *Usonia*, Samuel Butler's visionary book on a new America. He completely restructured the plan of the house, stripping it down to its essentials. By using materials that were self-finishing, such

Goetsch-Winkler House

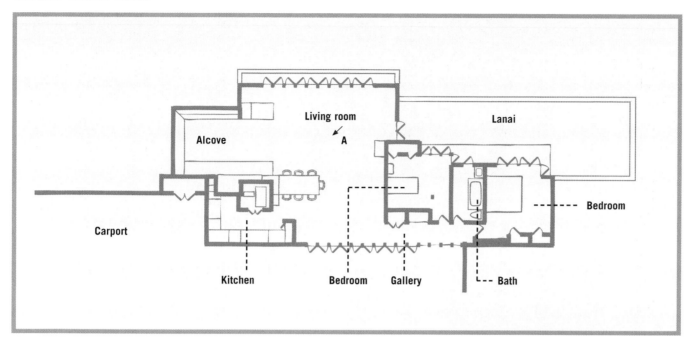

By rethinking the floorplan of the house, Wright eliminated the formal places of the house and integrated the kitchen with the living area. (Photo taken at A on floorplan.)

as brick, wood, and concrete, he helped revolutionize the building process. Unlike the Disney version, which boasted synthetic materials and ultramodern forms, Wright's vision incorporated human-scaled spaces created with natural materials. Wright's Usonian houses remain among the most successful interpretations of the house of the future.

The reason these houses have aged well is that they were designed for the human beings who live in them, not for the technology of the time. Wright, working in the 1930s and '40s, proposed the equivalent of the Not So Big House, putting emphasis on interior detail and livability rather than on quantity of space. Yet throughout the first half of the 20th century, many architects attempted to create futuristic houses that were often sleek, uncluttered, and completely impersonal. Many of these houses, although elegant in photographs, make uncomfortable homes. Perhaps one reason why the unadorned archi-

Designed for the people who lived in them, not for the technological fads of the time, Wright's Usonian houses have aged gracefully. This interior is filled with light and natural materials.

This elegant house was designed by Mies van de Rohe: A house of windows is a beautiful idea, but it's difficult to live in.

This apartment building, by French architect Le Corbusier, was designed to offer human-scaled living units made of precast concrete. Although the design was exciting to many architects of the day, to many of the inhabitants the apartments were cold and difficult to personalize.

tectural forms of the Modern movement have not been embraced is that people want to live in a place that can be either imprinted with their own personality or made to resemble their archetypal image of home. Despite the rhetoric of the Modernists that houses are machines for living, one incredibly important ingredient was left out of their designs: A house is a not an expression about society or technology; it's an expression of the people who live in it.

While Disneyland's House of Tomorrow predicted a totally synthetic environment, the charms of sitting on plastic chairs continue to elude most of us. Wood, or at least a composite made of wood, is far more comfortable. And with a new emphasis on sustainability and renewable materials, enormous numbers of recycled materials are entering the marketplace—from waterproof countertops made from recycled cardboard to interior trim made from wood scraps. These products are quite

The sleek, revolutionary form of the Villa Savoye, also designed by Le Corbusier, fell into disrepair within only a few decades. Its vision of a brave new world eluded the average homeowner, who sought a more familiar pattern of living.

Sustainability

Over the past few decades, there has been a growing awareness that as a society we have to redesign the systems that produce and support our way of life so that we don't continue to squander the earth's resources. This concept is known as sustainability. Before the Industrial Revolution, the only pollutants entering the thin layer of film around the earth came from the movement of the earth's crust, such as volcanoes and earthquakes. But over the past 200 years, that biosphere has been undeniably affected by the mining of fossil fuels. Nature's cleaning mechanisms, the green-celled plants that cover our planet, cannot keep up with the increase in pollutants.

In Sweden, an organization founded in 1985 by a group of concerned doctors and scientists put forth a proposal called the Natural Step. Prompted by a research oncologist's concerns about the increasing rate of cancer in children, the Natural Step teachings are based on scientific principles and put forth guidelines for how individuals, organizations, and companies can best meet the requisites of sustainability. Through a massive public-education campaign, Sweden has made huge strides toward a sustainable future. Many major corporations, such as Electrolux, Nike, Interface, and IKEA, have been inspired by the Natural Step guidelines and have adopted their own codes of sustainability.

Here in America, the ideas related to sustainable architecture are presented most eloquently by architect Bill McDonough, who is responsible for many of the most influential and interesting ideas about how to put our ecosystem back into balance. McDonough has tried to find ways to eliminate the concept of waste, and over the past 25 years he's moved from maverick to mainstream as people have begun to realize the importance of his message. Paul Hawken, another American visionary, also writes about the need for our economy to duplicate nature's cycles, in which the waste of one process becomes the food for another.

Recycled materials are transformed into "ShetkaBoard" blocks; this sample is made from recycled newspaper.

Sustainability does not mean that we should give up any of the hard-earned comforts that we have come to expect in the modern world. But, as with the design of the Not So Big House, we should evaluate what we really want and need and focus our attention on how to obtain these things by using fewer raw materials. To achieve a sustainable future, houses will need to be built according to these guidelines. Many of the concepts inherent in building Not So Big are the key to that future.

beautiful, exhibiting colors and textures all their own. Unlike plastic, they have innate personality. Like a beautiful piece of wood, they tell us something about their origins.

Building for Change

No one knows for certain what the house of the future will look like, but there's a good chance it will look more like a house we'd recognize as such and less like something from a science-fiction movie. What features will the house of the future have? If you can imagine the need for something, then there will be a solution. In house design today there are a number of revolutionary new products, ranging from smart house controls to insulation systems to construction technologies. Many of these products and processes will certainly have an impact on house design in the future, but they don't have to be the driving force behind the design. Rather, they will be integrated into our expectations of what a house should look like.

Given how rapidly technological change is occurring, it is crucial that we figure out a way to accommodate change without having to tear out and throw away substantial portions of the house in the process. For example, almost as soon as you install the latest audio/video system, it's out-of-date. And because there is no standardized way of getting at the mass of installed wires behind the walls, the system is very hard to replace. In an automobile we know where the spark plugs are and can change them with ease. Our houses need similar standard places where the "nervous system" can be easily accessed without having to tear apart walls and ceilings and rebuild major structural elements.

The house of the future is likely to be a house that evokes memories of our roots. The technology of the future needs to be integrated gracefully, not worn like a badge.

The house of the future will be designed so that unpredictable, changing technology can be integrated into the building without affecting the aesthetics. Since we cannot predict with any accuracy what the innovations of tomorrow will be, our strategies for integration must lie more in common sense than in clairvoyance and technical wizardry. We can be certain that conservation and maintainability are issues that will continue to have value. By designing our homes to be good custodians of our natural resources, and by engineering them to allow for ease of maintenance and future modification, we will be serving both ourselves and our planet well.

Simplify, Simplify, Simplify

There are many reasons, from aesthetic to practical, why the house of the future will be Not So Big. Families are getting smaller, an increasing proportion of the population has children who have left home, and there are more couples without children and more single home-owners. None of these groups requires the typical three- or four-bedroom house. In addition, many of these individuals, couples, and families are seeking something quite different in their lives. They are interested in simplifying, and in reallocating their time and personal resources to the things that give them pleasure and their lives a sense of meaning.

People are making conscious choices to reduce the number of activities they participate in, in order to reconnect with that part of themselves that might be termed "soul." Just take note of the flood of books about simplification to hit the bookstores over the past few years, such as *Simple Abundance*, by Sarah Ban Breathnach (Warner Books, 1995), *Kitchen Table Wisdom*, by Rachel Naomi Remen (Riverhead Books, 1996), and *Care of the Soul*, by Thomas Moore (HarperCollins, 1992). We crave a return to a more supportable pace and scale. Whether the simplification

The house of the future will include myriad special details, like this stained-glass window designed specifically for this spot.

comes in the form of reduced work hours or taking a few minutes a day for contemplation, people are making choices that allow them to become masters again of their own time.

To be surrounded by an environment that is both beautiful and personally enriching has far more appeal than the futile attempt to "keep up with the Joneses." When we have what the Joneses have, we experience firsthand the inadequacy of the dream. There is a deep yearning for something more. The paradox is that that something more resides in less. More quality, less quantity. More beauty, less bravado. More inner abundance, less outer display of wealth. The move toward a simpler way of living, and toward a re-alignment of our outer lives with our inner beliefs, leads along the same path as building Not So Big. Though we may not automatically name it as such, this move to do more with less arises from a generosity of spirit: a wish for sufficiency instead of overindulgence.

Reducing Waste

Primary in the move to sufficiency is the growing recognition that we cannot continue to squander the earth's resources at the current rate. By reducing the amount of waste we generate in the process of building homes, we will not only become

This house, built in a hot climate, was designed to minimize its use of energy and nonrenewable resources. Thick masonry walls and small windows protect the house against summer sun and associated heat gain.

better custodians of our planet but also improve the quality of life for generations to come.

Because a Not So Big House reduces the sheer quantity of space, it automatically reduces the quantity of materials. But even more important is the way such a house is built. The laptop computer on which this book was composed weighs only about 5 lb., yet the raw materials that went into its creation weighed 40,000 lb.! Similarly, the way houses are built is incredibly wasteful of resources. If you've ever driven by a construction site, you'll have seen the wasted materials, the wood and drywall, that fill the dumpsters. There are some basic strategies that our firm and other architects and builders across the country are embracing to help reduce the amount of waste. The first is the panelization of houses.

Panelization

In the panelization process, the envelope of the house is pre-built in panels in a factory setting. Almost any plan for any new house can be panelized. The process prevents an enormous amount of waste. Many panelization companies recycle literally everything into more building products. And panelization results in a better product. The control possible in the factory setting means that construction isn't stopped by bad weather, which can do serious damage to a house during the building process. In the construction of my own house, which was up and enclosed in four days, not one drop of rain or snow soaked into any of the building materials.

Panelization can take two principal forms. Structural insulated panels, known as SIPs, are made of two sheets of plywood, or oriented strand board, encasing a thickness of rigid insulation. These panels are very energy-efficient, and they are becoming increasingly popular for residential construction. The other form of panelization is the one you see in the photos on these two pages. The panels are made using regular stud-

This panelized house, with 2,400 sq. ft. of finished space and a two-car garage, went up in four days. It was fabricated by Sterling Building Systems over a seven-day period in a factory setting.

1. The trucks arrive, with the panels to be used first ready for unloading.
2. A crane helps unload panels and set them in place.
3.–5. By the afternoon of Day 1, all the main-floor framing is in place, complete with windows and plywood sheathing.
6. Day 2: The wall framing for the second floor and attic is in.
7. Day 3: The roof overhang is situated, and roof panels are positioned.
8. Day 4: The house is completely framed and enclosed.
9. The completed house (a few months later).

At the end of the erection process, the only waste was a tiny pile of strapping and spacer blocks used in shipping (photo bottom right).

Firmness, Commodity, and Delight

When Vitruvius, the first-century Roman statesman, proclaimed that our dwellings should offer "firmness, commodity, and delight," he was, in a way, advocating the Not So Big philosophy. It's almost as though, after World War II, we decided that we had to concentrate on structural stability and function in our houses but didn't have enough resources to allow for comfort and charm. Since then, size has been added to the equation, but precious little delight or commodity.

The Not So Big House puts commodity and delight back where they belong. And it does so by its very nature. With its functions streamlined to everyday activities and its architecture designed and tailored to the lives of those who live there, the Not So Big House celebrates the beauty of daily life. With minimum means, it makes the act of living an art. It restores the soul to the structure. Firmness, commodity, and delight—all at play together—turn a house into a home.

A beautiful composition of tiles graces the backsplash in an artfully designed kitchen.

frame construction, that, once installed, looks no different from any other framed house. The benefit of this type of panelization is that it requires no unusual installation techniques from electricians, plumbers, or other subcontractors. It also produces a very stable and tight house.

Within the next two decades it is likely that most of our homes will be fabricated in this manner. Just like an automobile, each house will be designed much more completely than houses are today, to include electrical, lighting, heating, cooling, security, and audio/video systems. With the use of computers and virtual reality to give potential buyers a walk-through of a model home before they build, the chances of repeating the experience of Paul and Laura, from Chapter 1, will be greatly diminished. Prospective homeowners will be able to "kick the tires," get a feel for the house, and get immediate cost feedback regarding their finish choices before they have committed to build a particular design. As with the automobile market, such direct visual feedback will allow us to make better use of our time and our money and will increase the design caliber of our homes in the process.

Recycled materials

In many instances, recycled materials can be as interesting as natural materials. Here in Minnesota, a company is turning junk mail into tile, old currency into countertops, and acres of pizza boxes into 1-ft.-square tiles that will adorn the walls of the newest Trump Tower in New York. The company (All Paper Recycling) calls the process "turning paper back into wood."

Recycled flooring materials are now available made from old soda bottles, recycled rubber and nylon cord, and carpet remnants. One product in use for many years—high-density fiberboard composed from wood scraps—is becoming a frequently used substitute for interior trim. Although it must be painted, it is an inexpensive and recycled product that, just like wood, can create interesting interior architecture.

There is a concern that the use of natural wood is bad for the environment and will become a thing of the past, but I don't believe this will happen. There are many ways to harvest trees as we do crops, and a movement called "sustainable harvest" is well under way. In Japan, where the wood resources are almost depleted, the use of wood veneer is a solution that allows interiors to still have the same aesthetic, but using much less raw material. A veneer is a thin slice of wood, typically $\frac{1}{36}$ in. thick, that is applied to a particleboard or plywood backing. A log that yields 100 sq. ft. of $\frac{3}{4}$-in. wall paneling could produce 3,500 sq. ft. of veneered paneling.

With the burgeoning interest in "green products" there are thousands of entrepreneurs around the country putting their imaginations to the task of creating new and interesting sustainable products. With such a plethora of new products, it's hard to predict what the standard construction materials of tomorrow will be. However, we can be sure that if the current awareness continues, these buildings will be made in an environmentally responsible way.

Energy-efficient construction

Energy efficiency continues to be an important issue for the future. Since the energy crisis of 1973, there's been a growing understanding of how to make our houses more energy-efficient. Houses built before that time tended to be leaky,

In this energy-efficient house, a two-story window wall on the south side lines the stairway and acts as a passive solar sunspace. Doors at the top and bottom of the stairs can be opened when the temperature within the sunspace rises above 70°F in the winter, bringing heat into the main living areas of the house.

letting outside air in and conditioned air out. In the past 25 years a lot of insulation has been added to the house's skin, better windows have been made, and air flowing in and out of the house has been controlled with a tighter air barrier. With this kind of energy-efficient house, there's a new and critical component to ensuring indoor air quality. This is an air-to-air heat exchanger that takes fresh air in, passes used air out, and transfers the heat from the outgoing air to the fresh air. Just as a house in a cold climate would never be built without a furnace or boiler today, the house of the future will not be constructed without an air-to-air heat exchanger, except in the most benign of climates. And as we continue to develop new ways to save energy, houses in colder climates will likely utilize some form of passive solar energy.

The pattern of light on a stair railing is one of those details you can't plan for. But when these guitar strings of light fall on the stair rail, they delight the home's inhabitants.

Hot climates create the same kind of energy demands as cold ones. So while there's currently less attention paid to insulation and air control in the houses in the South and Southwest than there is in the North, there should be. Insulation will keep the heat out, just as well as it can keep it in.

One of the challenges in building an energy-efficient house is how to maintain basic human requirements like access to light. Here in Minnesota there's a very stringent energy code, and because windows are the least energy-efficient component of a house's skin, the code attempts to limit the number of windows. Humans are incredibly light-sensitive—and in a colder climate, the quantity of light has a direct affect on the quality of life. How do we balance human needs with society's needs? If a code restricts something necessary to building a good house—such as windows—the market responds by inventing a better window. Rather than reducing the number of windows that we desire, the inventive minds of our time are coming up with solutions for windows that will allow us to let more light and views into our houses and still keep them energy-efficient. Although the technology is not yet readily available in the marketplace, there will be dramatic advances in window energy efficiency in the coming decade. Imagine windows that change from clear to opaque depending on the time of day, or windows in hot climates that help keep the house cooler.

For the long term, a house that is designed to make optimal use of the energy required to heat and cool it will be one that its future inhabitants are more likely to maintain. No matter what fuel prices do over the coming decades, a house that requires a lower amount of energy to sustain it is going to allow its residents to fare better than one requiring more. By looking

An experimental window turns from clear to opaque with the touch of a button. Within the next 10 years, window technologies like these will be commonplace.

further into the future and building for energy efficiency, we will be securing ourselves more comfortable and more environmentally supportable lives.

Building for the Future

We are slowly coming to understand that if we build for our short-term needs alone, with buildings that self-destruct in only a generation or two, there will continue to be no sense of past and no sense of soul. Our perspective is broadening. We are looking into the future and are starting to grapple with how we can help maintain our planet in the state of balance that we recognize as home.

Design and craft take time. They take time to learn, time to execute, and time to appreciate. But it is time that we seem to have lost in our fast-paced, information-drenched society. The paradox we confront is that our productivity has given us the wealth to acquire whatever we desire materially, but we are finding that material alone is an insufficient vision. The qualities we long for have everything to do with taking time, building for the long term, crafting and paying attention to who we are, what we care about, and how we affect our world. The Not So Big House is a home in every sense of the word. It is a place that, by its very nature, asks you to dwell there a while and to take in all that it offers.

The archetype of home is understood even by children, who always draw houses with gabled roofs and chimneys puffing a curlicue of smoke (see the drawing on the facing page). This image of home is ingrained in our imaginations, and it's not

The house of the future will feature art, craft, and design. We will make the house of the future uniquely our own, an expression of our true selves.

Our houses of the future won't look as though they just arrived from Mars. They'll be tailored to the way we really live, with each space used every day and filled with details that express our passions. More than anything, the house of the future will be both beautiful and comfortable.

suddenly going to be replaced by a space-age pod on Mars. The pattern is clear—revolutions in housing have traditionally been rejected and replaced by more familiar forms. The way the house of the future will look and feel is based on *evolution* not revolution. As technology evolves, the house of the future will integrate it into the existing familiar forms. The rate of technological change will continue to increase exponentially, but our homes will always be the "stillpoint," the resting place and secure haven of balance and comfort. The Not So Big House offers a way to bring the soul back into our homes, our communities, and our society's fabric. The house of the future will be Not So Big—and an expression of who we are and the way we really live.

Afterword

So how can we get there from here? How can we change our perceptions of what constitutes a good house and convince our friends and neighbors that we are not crazy for building smaller, more tailored homes that in all likelihood will cost just as much as their larger ones? I believe that the more people put their money where their hearts are, the more others will realize the validity of building for comfort, and not for prestige.

We should look more closely at ourselves, at how we want to live, at what inspires us, and at what our planet needs to return to balance. If we can start reflecting these values in our houses, we will make a small but significant step in helping humanity achieve the extraordinary spirit that all are born with. Over time we can too easily become jaundiced to the simple pleasures of existence, and our homes become just one more chore to maintain. What if instead they daily inspired us, filling us with feelings of appreciation for the richness that always surrounds us—if we only will look?

It can happen. I watch it happen with many of the new houses and additions we design. Past clients will call and report a sort of transport brought about by the new place they live in. Their houses are expressions of themselves, extensions almost, that they can share with friends and relatives, knowing that the house enriches not only their lives but all the lives that pass through it.

These houses have been designed and built with great care, and that care becomes a joyous presence in the completed home. Such a home is a place of great peace—one in which the residents can hear their own pulse and come to understand what makes them tick. I hope you will share this book with others you feel will appreciate and benefit from it. In a very real way, adopting the philosophy of house design espoused here can help fill a great void in our collective consciousness. We all want to go home, but we don't know how. This book, I hope, will help us find the way.

Bibliography

Alexander, Christopher, et al. *A Pattern Language: Towns, Building, Construction.* New York: Oxford University Press, 1977.

Anderson, Bruce, and Malcolm Wells. *Passive Solar Energy: The Homeowner's Guide to Natural Heating and Cooling* (2nd ed.). Amherst, N.H.: Brick House Publishing, 1994.

Ban Breathnach, Sarah. *Simple Abundance: A Daybook of Comfort and Joy.* New York: Warner Books, 1995.

Barrie, Thomas, and Gyorgy Doczi. *Spiritual Path, Sacred Place: Myth, Ritual, and Meaning in Architecture.* Boston: Shambhala Publications, 1996.

Brand, Stewart. *How Buildings Learn: What Happens after They're Built.* New York: Viking, 1994.

Brown, Azby. *Small Spaces: Stylish Ideas for Making More of Less in the Home.* New York: Kodansha, 1993.

Harwood, Barbara Bannon. *The Healing House.* Carlsbad, Calif.: Hay House, 1997.

Hawken, Paul. *The Ecology of Commerce: A Declaration of Sustainability.* New York: Harper Business, 1994.

Hermannsson, John. *Green Building Resource Guide.* Newtown, Conn.: The Taunton Press, 1997.

Lawlor, Anthony. *A Home for the Soul: A Guide for Dwelling with Spirit and Imagination.* New York: Clarkson Potter, 1997.

Lulic, Margaret A. *Who We Could Be at Work.* Newton, Mass.: Butterworth-Heinemann, 1996.

Marcus, Clare Cooper. *House as a Mirror of Self: Exploring the Deeper Meaning of Home.* Berkeley, Calif.: Conari Press, 1995.

Marinelli, Janet, and Robert Kourik. *The Naturally Elegant Home: Environmental Style.* New York: Little, Brown, 1992.

Moore, Charles. *The Place of Houses.* New York: Henry Holt, 1979.

Moore, Thomas. *Care of the Soul.* New York: HarperCollins, 1992.

Moore, Thomas. *Soul Mates.* New York: HarperCollins, 1994.

Papanek, Victor. *The Green Imperative: Natural Design for the Real World.* New York: Thames and Hudson, 1995.

Pye, David. *The Nature and Aesthetics of Design.* New York: Van Nostrum Reinhold, 1978.

Pye, David. *The Nature and Art of Workmanship.* New York: Cambridge University Press, 1968.

Stevens, Peter S. *Patterns in Nature.* Boston: Atlantic–Little, Brown, 1974.

Traditional Neighborhood Designs. St. Paul, Minn.: HomeStyles Publishing, 1997.

Tremblay, Kenneth Jr., and Lawrence Von Bamford (Eds.). *Small House Designs.* Pownal, Vt.: Storey, 1997.

Credits

PAGE 75 (TOP)
Architect: Sarah Susanka &
James R. Larson
Photographer: Sarah Susanka

PAGE 75 (BOTTOM)
Architect: Sarah Susanka, MSMP
Photographer: Sarah Susanka

PAGE 76 (TOP)
Architect: Kelly Davis with
Timothy Old, MSMP
Photographer: Karen Melvin

PAGE 76 (BOTTOM)
Designer: Laurel Ulland, MSMP
Photographer: Phillip Mueller

PAGE 77
Architect: Sarah Susanka &
Michaela Mahady, MSMP
Photographer: Karen Melvin

PAGE 78 (TOP)
Architect: Kelly Davis with Timothy
Old, MSMP
Photographer: Karen Melvin

PAGE 78 (BOTTOM)
Architect: Sarah Susanka &
James R. Larson
Photographer: Jeff Krueger

PAGE 79 (TOP)
Architect: Sarah Susanka &
James R. Larson
Photographer: Christian Korab

PAGE 79 (BOTTOM)
Architect: Sarah Susanka with Ollie
Foran, MSMP
Photographer: Christian Korab

PAGE 80
Architect: Sarah Susanka &
James R. Larson
Photographer: Christian Korab

PAGE 81
Architect: Sarah Susanka with
James R. Larson, MSMP
Photographer: Sarah Susanka

PAGE 82
Architect: John Calvin Womack
Photographer: *Fine Homebuilding*
(© The Taunton Press, Inc.)

PAGE 83 (LEFT)
Architect: Sarah Susanka &
James R. Larson
Photographer: Christian Korab

PAGE 83 (RIGHT)
Architect: Timothy Fuller, MSMP
Photographer: Christian Korab

PAGES 84, 85
Architect: Dale Mulfinger &
Timothy Fuller, MSMP
Photographer: Karen Melvin

PAGE 86
Architect: Sarah Susanka with
M. Christine Johnson, MSMP
Photographer: Chris Ostlind

PAGE 87
Architect: Dale Mulfinger with
Mark Malaby, MSMP
Photographer: Peter Kerze

PAGES 88, 89
Architect: Sarah Susanka with
Steven Mooney, MSMP
Photographer: Jeff Krueger

PAGE 90
Architect: Sarah Susanka with
James R. Larson, MSMP
Photographer: Christian Korab

PAGE 91
Architect: John Ferro Sims
Photographer: John Ferro Sims

PAGE 92 (TOP)
Architect: Sarah Susanka, MSMP
Photographer: Christian Korab

PAGE 92 (BOTTOM)
Designer: Philip S. Sollman
Photographer: Philip S. Sollman

PAGE 93 (LEFT)
Architect: Todd Remington
Photographer: Steve Culpepper
(© The Taunton Press, Inc.)

PAGE 93 (RIGHT)
Architect: Janet Moody
Photographer: Scott Gibson
(© The Taunton Press, Inc.)

PAGE 94 (LEFT)
Architect: Tony Simmonds
Photographer: Charles Miller
(© The Taunton Press, Inc.)

PAGE 94-95
Photographer: Charles Miller
(© The Taunton Press, Inc.)

PAGE 95 (RIGHT)
Architect: Dale Mulfinger &
Cheryl Fosdick, MSMP
Photographer: Karen Melvin

PAGE 96
Designer: John Hermannsson
Photographer: John Hermannsson

PAGE 97 (LEFT)
Architect: Sarah Susanka &
James R. Larson
Photographer: Crystal Kitchens

PAGE 97 (RIGHT)
Architect: Sarah Susanka with
M. Christine Johnson, MSMP
Photographer: Sarah Susanka

PAGE 98 (LEFT)
Architect: Kelly Davis with
Timothy Old, MSMP
Photographer: Karen Melvin

PAGE 98 (RIGHT)
Architect: Michaela Mahady &
Paul Buum
Photographer: Christian Korab

PAGE 99
Designer: Fu Tung Cheng
Photographer: Charles Miller
(© The Taunton Press, Inc.)

PAGE 100
Architect: Sarah Susanka with
James Larson, MSMP
Photographer: Susan Gilmore
(© Meredith Corp.)

PAGES 101-104
Architect: Kelly Davis
Photographer: Karen Melvin

PAGES 105-107
Architect: Kelly Davis
Photographer: *Fine Homebuilding*
(© The Taunton Press, Inc.)

PAGES 108-109, 111-112
Architect: Sarah Susanka with
James R. Larson, MSMP
Photographer: Susan Gilmore
(© Meredith Corp.)

PAGES 114-117
Architect: Michaela Mahady
& Wayne Branum, MSMP
Photographer: George Heinrich

PAGE 119-121
Architect: Michaela Mahady
& Wayne Branum, MSMP
Photographer: Christian Korab

PAGE 123
Architect: Tony Simmonds
Photographer: Charles Miller
(© The Taunton Press, Inc.)

PAGE 125
Architect: Dale Mulfinger with
Mark Malaby, MSMP
Photographer: Peter Kerze

PAGES 126, 128-131
Architect: Kelly Davis with
Timothy Old, MSMP
Photographer: Lark Gilmer

PAGE 132
Architect: Victoria Holland
Photographer: Andrew Wormer
(© The Taunton Press, Inc.)

PAGE 133
Architect: Michaela Mahady
Photographer: Philip Mueller

PAGE 134 (LEFT)
Architect: Sarah Susanka with
Richard Peterson, MSMP
Photographer: Kevin Ireton
(© The Taunton Press, Inc.)

PAGE 134 (RIGHT)
Architect: Robert Gerloff
Photographer: John Danicic

PAGE 137
Architect: Joseph G. Metzler with
Steven Buetow, MSMP
Photographer: Susan Gilmore

PAGE 138
Photographer: Reese Hamilton
(© The Taunton Press, Inc.)

PAGE 139
Architect: Sarah Susanka, MSMP,
with Paul Hannan, MSMP
Photographer: Christian Korab

PAGE 140
Photographer: Steve Culpepper
(© The Taunton Press, Inc.)

PAGE 141
Photographer: Roe A. Osborn
(© The Taunton Press, Inc.)

PAGE 142-146
Architect: Sarah Susanka, MSMP,
with Paul Hannan, MSMP
Photographer: Christian Korab

PAGE 146 (BOTTOM)
Architect: Dale Mulfinger &
Sarah Susanka, MSMP
Photographer: Sarah Susanka

PAGE 148
Architect: Sarah Susanka &
James R. Larson
Photographer: Sarah Susanka

PAGE 149-152, 153 (TOP)
Architect: Kelly Davis, MSMP
Photographer: Christian Korab

PAGE 153 (BOTTOM)
Architect: Kelly Davis, MSMP
Photographer: Sarah Susanka

PAGE 154, 156, 157 (TOP)
Architect: Kelly Davis, MSMP
Photographer: Christian Korab

PAGE 157 (BOTTOM), 158 (TOP
& BOTTOM LEFT)
Architect: Kelly Davis, MSMP
Photographer: Sarah Susanka

PAGE 158 (RIGHT)
Architect: Kelly Davis, MSMP
Photographer: Christian Korab

PAGE 159
Architect: Joseph G. Metzler with
Steven Buetow, MSMP
Photographer: Susan Gilmore

PAGE 160
Architect: Sarah Susanka with
Richard Peterson, MSMP
Photographer: Kevin Ireton
(© The Taunton Press, Inc.)

PAGE 161, 162 (TOP)
Architect: Sarah Susanka with
James R. Larson
Photographer: Christian Korab

PAGE 162 (BOTTOM)
Architect: Joseph G. Metzler, MSMP
Photographer: Bruce Greenlaw
(© The Taunton Press, Inc.)

PAGE 163
Architect: Michaela Mahady &
Wayne Branum, MSMP
Photographer: George Heinrich

PAGE 164
Architect: Sarah Susanka with
Richard Peterson, MSMP
Photographer: Karen Melvin

PAGE 165 (TOP)
Architect: Michaela Mahady with
M. Christine Johnson, MSMP
Photographer: Christian Korab

PAGE 165 (BOTTOM)
Architect: Sarah Susanka, MSMP
Photographer: Sarah Susanka

PAGE 166
Architect: Sarah Susanka &
Michaela Mahady, MSMP
Photographer: Karen Melvin

PAGES 167, 169-171
Architect: Michaela Mahady with
M. Christine Johnson, MSMP
Photographer: Phillip Mueller

PAGE 172 (LEFT)
Architect: Sarah Susanka with
Richard Peterson, MSMP
Photographer: Karen Melvin

PAGES 172 (RIGHT), 173
Architect: Joseph G. Metzler with
Steven Buetow, MSMP
Photographer: Susan Gilmore

PAGE 174
Architect: Michaela Mahady &
Wayne Branum, MSMP
Photographer: George Heinrich

PAGE 175
Architect: Sarah Susanka &
James R. Larson
Photographer: Sarah Susanka

PAGE 176 (TOP)
Architect: Claude-Nicolas Ledoux

PAGE 176 (MIDDLE)
Architect: Buckminster Fuller
Photographer: Balthazar Korab

PAGE 176 (BOTTOM)
Photographer: Balthazar Korab

PAGE 177
Architect: Alfredo DeVido
Photographer: Joanne Kellar
Bouknight (© The Taunton
Press, Inc.)

PAGES 178-180
Architect: Frank Lloyd Wright
Photographer: Balthazar Korab

PAGE 181 (TOP LEFT)
Architect: Mies Van der Rohe
Photographer: Hedrich Blessing

PAGE 181 (TOP & BOTTOM RIGHT)
Architect: Le Corbusier
Photographer: Balthazar Korab

PAGE 182
Photographer: Christian Korab

PAGE 183
Architect: Michaela Mahady &
Wayne Branum, MSMP
Photographer: George Heinrich

PAGE 184
Architect: Dale Mulfinger &
Sarah Susanka, MSMP
Photographer: Dale Mulfinger

PAGE 185
Architect: Peter L. Pfeiffer
Photographer: Steve Culpepper
(© The Taunton Press, Inc.)

PAGE 186-187
Architect: Sarah Susanka &
James R. Larson
Photographer: James R. Larson

PAGE 188
Designer: Laurel Ulland, MSMP
Photographer: Sarah Susanka

PAGE 189
Architect: Dale Mulfinger with
Sam Alexander, MSMP
Photographer: Dale Mulfinger

PAGE 190
Architect: Sarah Susanka &
James R. Larson
Photographer: Sarah Susanka

PAGE 191
Architect: Sarah Susanka with
Ollie Foran, MSMP
Photographer: Christian Korab

PAGE 192
Architect: Kelly Davis, MSMP
Photographer: Karen Melvin

PAGE 193 (TOP)
Architect: Sarah Susanka &
James R. Larson
Photographer: Christian Korab

PAGE 193 (BOTTOM)
Artist: Greyson Babcock

Index

Visit *The Not So Big House* online at: www.notsobighouse.com.

Publisher JIM CHILDS

Acquisitions Editor JULIE TRELSTAD

Assistant Editor KAREN LILJEDAHL

Editors PETER CHAPMAN, STEVE CULPEPPER

Designer SUZANNE NOLI

Layout Artist JODIE DELOHERY

Illustrator SCOTT BRICHER

Typeface GOUDY

Printer R. R. DONNELLEY, WILLARD, OHIO

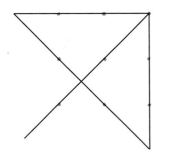